ISRAEL IN THE NEW TESTAMENT

ISRAEL IN THE NEW TESTAMENT

David Pawson

Terra Nova Publications

Published in Great Britain by
Terra Nova Publications International Ltd.
Orders and enquiries: PO Box 2400 Bradford on Avon BA15 2YN
Registered Office (not for trade): 21 St. Thomas Street, Bristol BS1 6JS

The views and opinions expressed in this book are those of the author,
and must not be taken to express those of the publisher,
wholesaler(s), booksellers or other distributors.

Cover design by Roger Judd

ISBN 978 1 901949 69 8

Printed in Great Britain by
CPI Bookmarque, Croydon

Contents

INTRODUCTION

Those who believe what the Bible teaches about God's plans and purposes for the people and place of Israel are often accused of giving more time and attention to the Old Testament than the New. They are criticised for taking prophetic promises of Israel's restoration and return to the promised land too literally, whereas most Christians take them metaphorically and apply the predicted blessings (though not the curses!) to the church. In addition, some are said to be historical (referring to the return from exile in Babylon) and others are said to be conditional (requiring a repentance not yet forthcoming).

Behind these charges lies the settled conviction that the Israel of the Old Testament has been 'replaced by' or 'fulfilled in' the Church of the New. This new body may contain a minority of Jews, alongside the Gentile majority. It may even become a larger proportion one day. But the Jewish nation as a whole is no longer God's chosen people and must be regarded, treated and judged like any other. The Jews as such no longer have a place in the plans and purposes of God.

If this were an accurate assessment of the situation, one would expect a fading significance of Israel in the New Testament. It comes as a surprise that the name 'Israel' is mentioned over seventy times, always with an ethnic meaning: the Jewish people. Furthermore, there is as much about Israel's future destiny as about her historic past, especially in the pages of the final book. Israel and the church have a parallel existence until the day they merge into one flock under one Shepherd, ultimately 'one new humanity' in *Yeshua HaMashiach*, Jesus the Christ.

This book is about Israel in the New Testament, or at least in five books of it. Originally given as a series of talks at the annual celebrations of the Feast of Tabernacles (organised by the International Christian Embassy in Jerusalem, and attended by thousands of believers from over a hundred countries), some of the chapters betray a spoken rather than a written style. Their enthusiastic reception suggested they would be welcome in a more permanent form.

For a more theological presentation of the stance for Israel in these pages, readers are commended to study my *Defending Christian Zionism*, which I regard as a companion to the present volume.

I believe that Israel has a future in God's purposes; that he has not finished with Israel; that neither the people nor the place have been left behind in God's purposes.

As always, I ask the reader to compare everything I say or write with what is written in the Bible and, if at any point a conflict is found, always to rely upon the clear teaching of scripture.

David Pawson

1

ISRAEL IN MATTHEW

On one occasion when I was visiting the holy land, I talked with a Jewish man who was doing research into what he found a very puzzling phenomenon — that so many Christians are interested in Israel. He told me that he had read the New Testament five times and found it full of anti-Israel material, so he wondered why Christians would be so concerned. We will be looking at certain books of the New Testament to see what they say about Israel. First, we are going to look at the Gospel of Matthew. Of the four Gospels, it is the only one that is primarily addressed to Jewish believers. That is why it is of interest to us in this study.

THE GOSPEL FOR JEWISH BELIEVERS

I want to give you at least seven reasons why we believe that this Gospel was written for Jewish believers. The first is that Matthew begins with the genealogy or family tree of Jesus. Now, if you were writing a Gospel for Gentiles and you wanted to capture their interest on the first page, you would not begin with the genealogy. It reads like the telephone directory, and is not going to grab your attention. Luke, writing for Gentiles, also includes the family tree of Jesus, but he puts it into chapter three so that he has your interest before you come to it. But to a Jew the family tree of Jesus is of vital interest. Years ago, I preached my way through Matthew chapter one, the family tree, and lo and behold, a Jewish man who was present came to faith in *Yeshua HaMashiach* through the genealogy. He said, 'For the first time, I realised *Yeshua* was a real person and that he was the Son of David.'

The second reason we believe this Gospel was written for Jewish believers is that there is so much from the Old Testament in Matthew, far more than in Mark or Luke or John. Matthew picks up strand after strand of the Hebrew scriptures, and I have the feeling that that is why it has been put first in the New Testament. It is the nearest to the Old Testament of the four Gospels, and it picks up all these threads. In particular, Matthew has a favourite word: 'fulfilled'. 'That it might be fulfilled, that was written in the prophet.' So he sees the prophets of the Old Testament fulfilled in the life of Jesus. Twelve times he uses that expression, and not only are the prophets fulfilled in Matthew but the law is also fulfilled. Jesus said, *"Do not think that I have come to abolish the Law or the Prophets; I have not come to abolish them but to fulfil them"* (Matthew 5:17, *NIV*).

If you want a simple definition of 'fulfil', it means: to get it done, to turn words into deeds, to bring about the reality of it. What are words in the prophets and the law become deeds and events in the life of Jesus. He came to make the Old Testament happen, turning the words of God into deeds.

Thirdly, I trust you know that Jews have a fear of using the name of the Lord in vain. Remember the second Commandment of the ten? That is why in the *Jerusalem Post* or any printed material you will never see the word 'God'. You will see G-d. Just in case they take the name of God in vain. Often they use a euphemism instead of 'God', and one of those euphemisms is 'heaven'. 'Pray to heaven, heaven will help you.' That may be the origin of the phrase in English 'heaven help you.' Throughout Matthew's Gospel, you do not find the phrase 'kingdom of God', which you will find everywhere in Mark and Luke, and even in John. You find the phrase 'the kingdom of heaven'. Once again, we find that Matthew has Jewish readers in mind, so with great tact he talks about the kingdom of heaven, rather than the kingdom of God, and we know it is simply a synonym because exactly the same things are said in the other Gospels about the kingdom of God that are said here about the kingdom of heaven.

The fourth thing we notice about this Gospel is that Matthew, who began as a collector of taxes and then became a collector of Jesus' teaching, has grouped the sayings of Jesus into five blocks. There are five great sermons in the Gospel of Matthew about the kingdom of heaven, and I will just run briefly through them. In Matthew chapters 5 – 7, we have what we call the Sermon on the Mount, and that is about the *lifestyle* of the kingdom, how we are to live. The second group of sayings about the kingdom of heaven is in chapter ten, and we can call that 'the *mission* of the kingdom' — how we are sent out, and what we are to do when we are sent out. Then, in chapter thirteen, we have another collection of sayings, about the *growth* of the kingdom of heaven — growth from a tiny mustard seed to a great tree the birds can come and nest in. The next section is in chapter eighteen, where it talks about the *community* of the kingdom of heaven, the church, and how we are to behave in the church, which Jesus came to build. Finally, in chapters 24–25, which we shall look at below, we have the *future* of the kingdom of heaven, and what is going to happen at the end of time. So we have five blocks of teaching collected by Matthew from Jesus' sayings. Is this not interesting? It seems that Matthew is almost subconsciously reflecting the *Torah*, our five books of Moses. And of course Jesus' pulpits were mountains. God provided those mountains in creation for Jesus to use as pulpits, and the first of these five sermons is on a mountain — we call it the Sermon on the Mount. But the last sermon

14

is as well. Chapters 24 and 25 are set on the Mount of Olives. Jesus loved to go up a mountain to give this teaching, and of course Moses went up Mount Sinai to receive his revelation from God. So there is an echo of the five books of Moses in the five sermons in the Gospel of Matthew.

The fifth thing is that Matthew mentions the name 'Israel' twelve times. That is more than any of the others; Mark's Gospel only mentions the word 'Israel' twice, and even John only five times. Now, we assume that Matthew took over the Gospel of Mark and expanded it by adding these blocks of Jesus' sayings. It means that Matthew has added the name 'Israel' ten times to the document he was using to base his Gospel on, namely Mark, who only used it twice.

The sixth point I want to mention is rather unusual. Mark and Luke, written for Gentiles, both give an absolute prohibition on divorce and remarriage. They both quote Jesus saying that if anyone divorces his wife and marries another he is committing adultery, and if anyone marries someone who has been divorced they are committing adultery — they are breaking that commandment. No exceptions, categorical statement, absolute prohibition, in Mark and Luke. But when we come to Matthew there is one exception to that rule, and that is a surprise. Why is that exception only in Matthew? Why is it not in Mark and Luke as well? We must try and find an explanation for this, and the explanation is that Jesus is speaking and Matthew is writing to Jewish believers who are familiar with both the Jewish culture and the Jewish law. I must explain two things about the Jewish law and culture. First, betrothal is as serious as being married. With us, an engagement is often a provisional thing that can be broken, but in Jewish culture, if you were engaged to be married, that was settled. You are as good as married, apart from the ceremony itself and the physical consummation. The other thing you need to know about Jewish culture is that the law demanded virginity of the bride. I always feel that was a bit unfair, but then if all the girls remained virgins that would prevent the men from losing their virginity as well. But nevertheless, the law stated that if a bride was not a virgin at her wedding she must be put to death. You will find this in Deuteronomy 22. By the time of Jesus, the death penalty had given way to the milder penalty of divorce. In other words, if your bride is not a virgin then you *must* divorce. It was a categorical imperative.

Now, it is very interesting that in the exception Jesus does not use the word 'adultery', which in Greek is the word *moicheia*. He uses the word *porneia*, fornication, and when those two words appear together, adultery is illicit sex after marriage, but fornication is illicit sex before marriage, and the exception therefore, I believe, in consistency with the Jewish law and culture — the only exception Jesus allowed — was illicit sex before marriage. And that, of course, is why Matthew records that even Jesus' parents nearly divorced on that ground. Joseph thought Mary has been promiscuous — it was thought that she must have been or she would not be pregnant — and being a just man he resolved to divorce her. But being a good man, he also resolved to do it privately and not publicly, to avoid her humiliation and disgrace. That was an example of the exception which Jesus here allows.

Quite frankly, it means that there is no exception for anything that happens after marriage in our New Testament. But the interesting thing, and the explanation as to why the only exception occurs in Matthew, is that he is acknowledging the Jewish culture and, indeed, the Mosaic law in Deuteronomy 22.

I could have given you far more reasons why we believe Matthew is written to Jewish believers, but the final one I will give you here is that, in this Gospel, Jesus is born king of the Jews and dies king of the Jews — the only Gospel that says both. You remember when the Wise Men came seeking Jesus? They said, *"Where is the one who has been born king of the Jews?"* And they were directed to royal David's city of Bethlehem. And then at the end, when a person was crucified, their crime was put on a board which was nailed to the cross above their head, 'Murderer', 'Thief', 'Zealot', whatever. Over Jesus' head was written THIS IS JESUS, THE KING OF THE JEWS.

Matthew alone says that he was born king of the Jews, and died king of the Jews.

That is enough, I hope, to persuade you that we are right in assuming that Matthew's Gospel was written for Jewish believers primarily. Of course, much in it also applies to us, but it is a reminder that the early churches, especially in Judaea, were Jewish congregations. Our church began with twelve Jewish apostles, and the early converts were Jewish. Thousands of them in the city of Jerusalem, including many priests, became believers in *Yeshua HaMashiach*. Matthew was written for these Jewish churches and congregations, but we are grateful to him for recording so much of our Lord's teaching.

SHEPHERD OF ISRAEL

Let us move on to look at some of the texts in which Matthew uses the word 'Israel'. The first is in connection with the visit of the Wise Men to Bethlehem. Some people say they were Gentiles, I believe they were Jews who had stayed behind in Babylon. Only a minority of the Jews came back after the exile, and I believe that many Jews stayed on, and they knew a prophecy that you will find in the book of Numbers in connection with Balaam, the man whose donkey put him right. One of the prophecies is that a star will arrive in Judah, a star that will carry the sceptre, the symbol of kingly rule. They were looking for the star, and they saw it, and they came all that way from Babylon, modern

Iraq. They arrived, enquiring about the one who has been born king of the Jews, and Herod was told of the prophecy of Micah,

"But you, Bethlehem, in the land of Judah,
are by no means least among the rulers of Judah;
for out of you will come a ruler
who will be the shepherd of my people Israel."

Matthew 2:6, *NIV*

Does that statement shock you? It ought to. A ruler is at the top of the social ladder. The king is the very peak of society, but the shepherd is at the bottom. We have a romantic view of shepherds, but in the ancient world the shepherd was at the bottom of the social ladder.

Remember when Samuel went to look at the sons of Jesse to see which one God had chosen as king, he saw them all and he said, *"The* LORD *has not chosen these . . . . Are these all the sons you have?"*

"There is still the youngest," Jesse answered, *"but he is tending the sheep"* (1 Samuel 16:10f., *NIV*). The youngest, sent out to do the dirty work for everybody else — only the shepherd boy.

It is remarkable that in the Bible ruler and shepherd should be brought together in the same person. It speaks of the majesty and the meekness of our Lord Jesus, Ruler and Shepherd of Israel. That theme is taken up in the rest of Matthew time and again. Jesus talks of the lost sheep of the house of Israel; he came looking for them, and, if I may jump ahead a little, on two occasions Jesus made it absolutely clear that his Heavenly Father had told him not to go to the Gentiles, not even the half-breed Samaritans, half-Jewish, half-Gentile. *"I was sent only to the lost sheep of Israel."* It was the Father's mandate to the Son. He came to be the Shepherd of Israel, and we forget that at our peril. All Jesus' ministry was directed to Israel.

There were two occasions when people who were not of the lost sheep of Israel came with remarkable faith to Jesus. One was a Roman centurion in Capernaum who came to Jesus asking for help.

"Lord," he said, "my servant lies at home paralysed and in terrible suffering."

Jesus said to him, "I will go and heal him."

The centurion replied, "Lord, I do not deserve to have you come under my roof. But just say the word and my servant will be healed. For I myself am a man under authority, with soldiers under me. I tell this one, 'Go,' and he goes; and that one, 'Come,' and he comes. I say to my servant, 'Do this,' and he does it."

When Jesus heard this, he was astonished and said to those following him, "I tell you the truth, I have not found anyone in Israel with such great faith."

Matthew 8:5ff., *NIV*

What a shock it must have been, and what a temptation to Jesus. Here was a Roman, showing more faith
than any one of the lost sheep of Israel.

The other occasion, of course, is up in the region of
Tyre and Sidon, with a Canaanite woman who had a
demon-possessed daughter. (15:21ff.) We do not know
what all the symptoms were, but it was serious. She
came to Jesus, and said, *"Lord, Son of David, have
mercy on me!"* Then she told him about her daughter.
And the astonishing thing is that Jesus said nothing to
her. The woman kept following them, calling out. She
was a pest, and finally the disciples asked Jesus to send
her away. Jesus was not sent to Canaanite women, and
he was keeping strictly to the mandate that his Father
had given him. He was the model of an obedient son.
When she knelt before Jesus and said, *"Lord, help
me!"* he finally said to her, *"It is not right to take the
children's bread and toss it to their dogs."* This is one
of those statements Jesus made that not many preachers
like to preach about. It seems not a very 'nice' thing to
have said. But her faith was such that she said, *"Yes,
Lord, but Lord, even the dogs eat the crumbs that
fall from their masters' table."* What faith! So he did
heal her daughter. But do you realise why he initially
refused to speak to her? He was obeying his Father,
and he would not commit an act of disobedience. And
it was on that occasion that he said, *"I was sent only
to the lost sheep of Israel."*

When Jesus sent out the disciples two by two, he did not send them to the Gentiles. Galilee particularly was 'Galilee of the nations' and it was full of Gentiles, but he told the disciples not to go to them — nor were they to go to the Samaritans, but only to the lost sheep of the house of Israel.

MIRACLES OF THE MESSIAH

This is rarely preached and rarely thought about. We think of Jesus healing the sick and raising the dead and causing the lame to walk and so on, but we think he just did it for anybody. No, he limited it to the house of Israel, and only on those two occasions, as far as we know, did he venture outside the lost sheep of Israel. He kept to his Father's orders, and we need to remember that Jesus came primarily for Israel. He was sent to Israel, and Matthew underlines that truth for us. Other Gospels, of course, underline it too, but Matthew particularly points it out.

Do you realise what a temptation it could have been to Jesus to disobey the Father and go to the Gentiles, when he could find such faith outside Israel? John's Gospel records an occasion, when Jesus was coming up to Jerusalem to die. A deputation came to Jesus from the north of the country, the area called the Decapolis, ten Greek cities on the eastern shore of Galilee. The Greeks came to Jesus and asked him to come to them and minister among them. There can be little doubt that the Greeks would really have responded to Jesus when the Jews did not. But Jesus knew what the Father had told him to do, and he stayed within Israel right to the end of his life.

Let us move on to the critical question of the future of Israel. I believe that Israel has a future in God's purposes, that he has not finished with Israel; that neither the people nor the place have been left behind in God's purposes. That, of course, runs right across many Christians who believe what we call 'replacement theology', though they now have a new term for it, 'fulfilment theology', which holds that, because the church has fulfilled the purpose of Israel, Israel is obsolete. I do not believe that. The New Testament very clearly states that Israel has a future, and that God has a future for her. And Matthew makes that clear.

I point to four particular texts. The first is the one in which Jesus surprisingly teaches that Abraham, Isaac and Jacob are still alive. I have been to Hebron, before it was closed to tourists, and have seen the so-called tombs of Abraham, Isaac and Jacob and their wives, in the building that is both a mosque and a church, and I was told that Abraham is buried there. His body may be there, but Abraham is not in Hebron, and Isaac is not, and nor is Jacob. We are told that God, the living God, *is* the God of Abraham and Isaac and Jacob, and they are very much alive. Some two thousand years after they had died, Jesus says they are still around.

He even said, *"Your father Abraham, rejoiced at the thought of seeing my day; he saw it and was glad"* (John 8:56, *NIV*). So I am convinced that the covenant God made with those three men, grandfather, father and son, is still valid. They are still alive, and if God has cancelled the covenant he has got to explain it to them, because they are still around.

FUTURE OF ISRAEL

Matthew moves on to reveal another astonishing thing: at the end of history, Abraham, Isaac and Jacob will all be there: *"I say to you that many will come from the east and the west, and will take their places at the feast with Abraham, Isaac and Jacob in the kingdom of heaven"* (Matthew 8:11, *NIV*). Here is Jesus speaking of the patriarchs of Israel, the forefathers of Israel who laid the foundation. They were not perfect men, but they were all men of faith, and they laid the foundation for God's people on earth, and on the basis of their faith God made covenants with all three. And we enjoy that covenant today. They are still around, the covenant is still around, nothing has changed in that regard.

The next verse I want to point to is 23:39, when Jesus says to Jerusalem, *"For I tell you, you will not see me again until you say, 'Blessed is he who comes in the name of the Lord'"* (*NIV*). If you drive up to Jerusalem from the airport, there is a huge sign in Hebrew as you reach the outskirts of Jerusalem, 'Blessed is he that comes'. It is a pity they did not quote the rest of the verse. Jesus was indicating that one day that city would welcome him back.

Finally, there is a verse in Matthew which by itself would be enough to support Christian Zionism: Jesus said, *"I tell you the truth, at the renewal of all things, when the Son of Man sits on his glorious throne, you who have followed me will also sit on twelve thrones, judging the twelve tribes of Israel"* (Matthew 19:28, *NIV*). The implications of that verse are enormous. First implication: there are no lost tribes of Israel. God has kept track of them all, and in fact it is foolish to talk about 'lost' tribes. I believe it is quite wrong to claim that Britain and America are those lost tribes. God, who can number the hairs on my head and knows the DNA of every individual, can trace them.

You may not have noticed in your Bible that when the ten tribes of the north were deported by Assyria, a number escaped deportation, and fled to the south, bringing with them remnants of the ten tribes who lived with Benjamin and Judah. In Israel, I asked one Jewish man if he was from the tribe of Manasseh, and he said he was not, but that people further east claimed to be of that tribe. I am sure the Lord knows where all the twelve tribes are, and he has promised to gather them all back. There will be representatives of all twelve tribes at the end of time.

God promised in Jeremiah:

> *This is what the LORD says,*
> *he who appoints the sun to shine by day,*
> *who decrees the moon and stars to shine by night,*
> *who stirs up the sea*
> *so that its waves roar—*
> *the LORD Almighty is his name:*
> *"Only if these decrees vanish from my sight,"*
> *declares the LORD,*
> *"will the descendants of Israel ever cease*
> *to be a nation before me."*
>
> Jeremiah 31:35f., *NIV*

So while the sun still shines and the waves roar, you know that Israel will still be here, and the twelve tribes will still be here, and the twelve apostles will be their judges, and each of them will look after one of the twelve tribes. We do have to say that of the twelve apostles one was lost and had to be replaced. Judas Iscariot was replaced by Matthias, but there will be twelve. And one of the twelve tribes was lost, the tribe of Dan. I am sure you know that they did not stay in the place that God chose for them, and they went north instead of west, and they chose their own place, and years later you can still see Jeroboam's altar up at Dan, where he raised the golden calf and tried to be a competitor of Jerusalem.

So one tribe was lost out of twelve, and one apostle out of twelve was lost. Both were replaced, in the one case by dividing the tribe of Joseph into two, and in the other case by casting lots and settling on Matthias. But at the end of history there will be twelve apostles judging twelve tribes of Israel. What could be clearer than that? If that were the only verse in Matthew that mentioned this, we would nevertheless have to believe that Israel has a future in God.

SOME MISINTERPRETED TEXTS

At this point we need to look at three passages in Matthew which have often been thought to refer to Israel, though the national name is not mentioned in any of them. They could turn out to be examples of *EISegesis* (reading *into* scripture what is not there) rather than *EXEgesis* (reading out of scripture what is there).

"Therefore I tell you that the kingdom of God will be taken away from you and given to a people who will produce its fruit" (Matthew 21:43, *NIV*).
This is a favourite text of those who believe that the church ('a people') has 'replaced' Israel ('you'). But the text needs to be seen in its setting.

The immediate context is the parable of the wicked tenants. When the landlord of the vineyard sends servants to collect the rent they are physically abused, some fatally. Finally sending his son, expecting him to be shown more respect, the very opposite happens.

As the only heir to the property, the tenants see an opportunity to seize it for themselves by expelling and executing him. Jesus is clearly predicting his own fate and referring to that of the prophets before him at the hands of their fellow Israelites. Cleverly, he invites his hearers to judge themselves and their predecessors by asking them what such an owner (clearly representing the God of Israel) should do with the tenants. They insist that a punishment should fit the crime (*"a wretched end for such wretches"*) but add advice about the vineyard, which should be transferred to trustworthy tenants. Jesus turns their moral indignation back on themselves (just as Nathan did to King David with *"you are the man"*, 2 Samuel 12:7) with *"will be taken from you"*.

But who does 'you' refer to? Obviously his hearers at least. Who were they? The answer is in v. 23. *The chief priests and the elders of the people*. In other words, the spiritual leaders of the nation, who regarded themselves as guardians of the 'kingdom' of Israel which they saw as the kingdom of God. They are to lose their position, forfeited by their rejection and assassination of him as the 'son' of God. Nothing is here said about the nation, only its leaders. We can agree that 'a people who will produce its fruit' refers to the future church, a new community of those who have accepted the 'son' rather than rejecting him. But it needs to be remembered that the initial 'tenants' would be all Jews, Gentiles only joining later. So the 'vineyard' was to be taken from some Jews and rented to other Jews.

"Now learn this lesson from the fig-tree: As soon as its twigs get tender and its leaves come out, you know that summer is near" (Matthew 24:32, *NIV*).

This time it is Christian Zionists who read 'Israel' into a text. It comes in the 'sermon on the mount' of Olives, in Jesus' answer to the question of his disciples about the 'signs' which will signal the approach of his 'second' coming. He cited four: disasters in the world; desertion in the church; dictatorship in the Middle East, and darkness in the sky. The order conveys a sense of increasing intensity and velocity. Each is accompanied by warnings of deception and counsels of reaction. In the summary of this part of his discourse, Jesus mentions the fig-tree as a 'sign' of approaching summer.

Taken as it stands, it is a simple *analogy*, illustrating discernment of any signs, as in the natural world. Jesus has done this before, referring to the well-known significance of red skies at night or in the morning (Matthew 16:1–2); he was contrasting his hearers' success in 'reading' nature and failure to discern the 'signs of the times'. The parallel case here is not a contrast but a comparison. Just as you know summer is near from signs in the fig-tree, 'even so' you will know that my coming is near, even 'at the door', when you 'see all these things' —that is, all the four signs he has explained in detail already, climaxing in the disappearance of sun, moon and stars.

However, some Zionists see the fig-tree as a complex *allegory*, rather than a simple analogy. Building on Old Testament usage of the tree as a metaphor for the people of Israel, and interpreting Jesus' cursing of a fruitless fig-tree as an acted parable of his disappointment with the nation, they assume the reference here is the same. But that involves giving a 'hidden' meaning to the tender twigs, blossoming buds and fruit leaves as the 'signs'. These are variously applied to the return of Jews to the promised land (from 1875), the establishment of the State of Israel (in 1948) or the recapture of the 'old' city of Jerusalem (in 1967). There are a number of reasons for doubting this explanation:

First, it is virtually adding a fifth 'sign' to those already given. Second, it distorts the chronological order of the signs, coming after the heavenly sources of light have been extinguished — so where does it fit into the sequence? Third, this view tends to distract from the four signs and stand on its own as the only precursor of the imminent return of the Lord, especially among 'dispensationalist' Zionists, who believe the four signs follow his return *for* his saints and will announce his later return *with* his saints. Fourth, and this seems to me conclusive, the parallel version of this passage in Luke's Gospel refers to 'the fig-tree and all the trees' (Luke 21:29); which would then mean the 'sign' (whatever it was) would be seen in all the (Gentile) nations, as well as Israel. Few seem to have noticed this. Our conclusion is that Jesus was talking about trees in general, not Israel in particular.

". . . whatever you did for one of the least of these brothers of mine, you did for me." (See Matthew 25:40–45).

This is often referred to as 'the parable of the sheep and the goats', but it is fact, not fiction; a prophecy rather than a parable. True, it begins with a simple analogy from the animal world. At the end of each day a shepherd would divide his flock, leaving the hardier goats out of doors and taking the more vulnerable sheep into a fold. But there the likeness with the day of judgement ends, for that separation will not be based on species but attitude and action. The thrust of Jesus' description depends on what he meant by 'my brothers'.

Liberal scholars broadly interpret 'brethren' in terms of the whole human race, based on our Lord's incarnation into our humanity. Their belief in God's universal Fatherhood inevitably implies the brother-hood of man. Any human being in need is both the brother of Jesus and mine, deserving 'family' asssistance. This view has been used to encourage thinking that 'do-gooders' are Christians, whether they are 'religious' or not, and even to support a 'gospel' of salvation by works. Christians themselves have used it to raise support for aid to victims of natural disasters, regardless of their faith. Certainly, Christians are called to 'do good to all people', but to assume Jesus means that here leads to moral and theological confusion.

At the opposite end of the spectrum, some Zionists narrowly interpret 'brethren' as Jesus' fellow Jews. Beginning with the Abrahamic covenant in which those who bless Israel will be blessed, and those who curse Israel will be cursed (Genesis 12:3) and noting the many prophetic judgements on Israel's enemies (e.g. Zechariah 9:1–8), the conclusion is drawn that there will be a special judgement day on those 'nations' who have opposed or persecuted the Jewish people (like Russia and Germany, for example). Note that 'nations' are taken as Gentiles and in a corporate sense as ethnic if not political entities, excluding Israel. Yet surely Jesus is referring to personal, even individual, acts of compassion rather than national policies. Did he ever call Jews his 'brothers'? Paul certainly did (Romans 9:3), though he qualified it by adding 'my kinsmen according to the flesh'.

When we ask how Jesus used 'brother', it seems that he used it in a spiritual sense. When told his brothers in his own family were waiting to see him, his response was: 'Who are my brothers?' Pointing to his disciples, he said, *"Here are . . . my brothers. For whoever does the will of my Father in heaven is my brother . . ."* (Matthew 12:48–50). Likewise, after his resurrection Jesus told the women running away from the empty tomb, *"Go and tell my brothers to go to Galilee; there they will see me"* (Matthew 28:10). In the light of these and other verses, it is extremely unlikely that Jesus was referring to the whole Jewish nation.

He was laying down an important principle, namely that actions (or inactions) towards his followers are virtually towards himself, whether that is consciously realised or not. Saul of Tarsus had to learn this truth. (*"I am Jesus, whom you are persecuting"*; Acts 9:5.) Jesus and his disciples are in such a union that they cannot be separated. It is impossible to love (or hate) one and not the other (1 John 3:17 and 4:20; note that both use 'brother' as a fellow-believer). In passing, note that when Jesus will say '*these* my brothers' he must be referring to a group present, probably pointing to them, presumably those already at his right hand. And to complete the picture, the goats at his left will include some Jews who have persecuted or neglected his disciples, yet unlike Paul, have never repented. So even the 'nation' of Israel will be divided on that day!

DEATH OF THE MESSIAH

It is time to return to our study of those passages in Matthew that directly relate to Israel, especially those connected with the crucifixion.

When we come to the death of Christ, we come to some very remarkable and serious mentions of Israel. The first text in Matthew to which I want to draw your attention is where Jesus said that the chief priests and teachers of the law would condemn him to death, but would turn him over to the Gentiles to be mocked, scourged and crucified. Again, if only the church for most of the last two thousand years had noticed that verse, it could have saved endless misunderstanding and worse. For much of that period the church of Christ has pointed to the Jew and said, 'You killed Jesus.' We had a Jewess in our church, a lovely Jewish woman who believed in *Yeshua*, but she was a little girl in Vienna, and when she was walking along the street and the Christian congregations came out, the Christian children would kick her and spit on her and say, 'You killed Jesus.' But this verse in Matthew is there to remind us all that Gentiles actually did the killing. Jews condemned him, but Gentiles mocked, scourged and crucified our Lord. So if anyone is going to say that 'You Jews killed Jesus', we ought to say immediately, 'And you Gentiles killed Jesus too.' In fact, of course, all of us were involved in the death of Jesus. He died for all of us, and therefore none of us can point to any other and say: you were responsible for the death of Jesus.

The next verse to which I draw your attention is the verse that quotes from Zechariah the prophet, a most unusual quotation: *That it might be fulfilled, they took the thirty silver coins, the price set on him by the people of Israel*. Now, that is a very puzzling statement. When you go back to Zechariah, you find that they rejected the prophet Zechariah as a bad shepherd, and they paid him off with thirty pieces of silver, and Zechariah felt insulted. Is that all that a prophet of God is worth to you? Matthew has taken up that incident, and seen in it a type of our Lord's own death. Thirty pieces of silver, that is peanuts, as we say. That is the value set on the life of Jesus by Israel, and it is very, very little. Judas sold him for that, and Zechariah, the prophet, felt so insulted at being paid off with thirty pieces of silver that he threw those coins at the potter, as directed by the Lord, and sure enough, in Judas' case, the thirty pieces of silver which he threw back, when he realised what he had done, were used to buy a potter's field down in the Valley of Gehenna.

We come then to this very, very serious prayer of the Jews who gathered in Pilate's courtyard when the trial of Jesus took place. It is a moving place. Do try to go there. In the old fortress of Antonia you can see the soldiers' games carved on the pavement; you can see the very courtyard on which Jesus stood. And the crowd shouted, *"Crucify him."* It was an extraordinary situation. Pilate, trying to ease his conscience, said, *"We have a custom of releasing a prisoner to you this time, shall I release Jesus?"* And he chose as the alternative a man called Jesus bar-Abbas, which means Jesus, or *Yeshua*, son of the father. Did you realise that was Barabbas's name? Here was Jesus the Son of the Father faced with Jesus 'son of the father', Jesus bar-Abbas, and they chose the freedom fighter or terrorist. And Jesus was crucified. Pilate wriggled, tried to escape his responsibility. He knew Jesus was innocent, but Pilate had a bad record of handling the Jews. When he stole the temple treasury to build an aqueduct there was such a riot, and Pilate's over-reaction was to crucify three thousand people. He was an ex-slave who had somehow gained his freedom, and when word of his mishandling of the Jews reached Rome he was told: one more mistake and you are out. So when he was faced with this difficult situation of Jesus and the Jews shouting for his crucifixion, he did everything he could to avoid sentencing him, even to finally washing his hands.

But the Jews present uttered this terrible prayer: *"His blood be upon us and our children."* Matthew records this. He wants the Jewish readers he is writing for to realise that they were responsible, and of course, even weeks after Jesus was crucified, Peter, preaching in this very city, said to the general population: *"You killed the author of life . . . "* (Acts 3:15); and, *"Therefore let all Israel be assured of this: God has made this Jesus, whom you crucified, both Lord and Christ"* (Acts 2:36, *NIV*). He had no hesitation in putting the responsibility on the population of Jerusalem. It is a fact that they demanded his crucifixion.

The final text that I want to refer to here is when Jesus hung on the cross and the public made fun of him. Now, in spite of all the crucifixes you have ever seen, Jesus was totally naked. It was the lot of a crucified person to be utterly humiliated and hung up, totally nude. I have only ever once seen a cross that portrays the truth in that regard, and it is a part of that extraordinary Cathedral of the Holy Family, in Barcelona. If ever you have seen that magnificent yet quite bizarre piece of architecture, there is, on one wall, a life-size crucifix of Jesus totally naked, totally humiliated, disgraced. They made fun of him, and one of the things they said on that occasion was: *"He is the King of Israel! Let him come down now from the cross"* — and the tragedy is that the Lord could have stepped off that cross so easily. He could have willed the nails out of his hands and feet, but he did not. He stayed there. Part of the mockery, and only Matthew records this, was: he is the King of Israel. You can paraphrase that as 'He is supposed to be the King of Israel,' and he was, but they did not realise it.

CALLING OF ISRAEL

We come to the final and most important point in this chapter: the final 'sermon on a mount'. It is found in Matthew chapter twenty-eight. It was the last time Jesus preached here on earth, and he had a congregation of five hundred. I want to draw your attention to these two facts. First, Jesus was, is and always will be, a Jew. We must never forget that. Second, all the congregation on this last occasion were Jews. Here is a Jew, speaking to five hundred Jews. And now he gives them a mandate totally opposite to the one he had received.

In John's Gospel, he says, *"As the Father sent me, so I send you."* The word for 'send' is in Greek the word *apostelein* or *apostelo*, from which we get our word 'apostle'. When the Bible was translated into Latin, the Greek word *apostelo* was changed into the Latin verb *mitto, mittere*, from which we get our words 'missile' and 'missionary'. Did you ever realise that a missionary is an intercontinental ballistic missile? Same word! Jesus uses this word — as I was *sent*, now I am *sending* you. The difference is this: when the Father sent Jesus — and Jesus was the first, the Chief Apostle, the one sent — he sent him only to Israel, and Jesus pretty well kept to that. He resisted the temptation to go to Samaritans, though he did once speak to a Samaritan woman, but he did not go there to preach or to heal. He did not go to the Gentiles, he kept to the Jews. But now, in the final 'sermon on the mount', he says, *"Go and make disciples of all the nations, baptising them and teaching them to observe all that I have commanded you."* It is the very opposite of Jesus' own mission. He was sent only to the lost sheep of the house of Israel. Now, he is sending Jews out into the world of Gentiles. The word 'nations' there does not mean political states, it is actually the word *ethne*. It means make disciples of all ethnic groups. That is my charge to you. I am sending you into the world of Gentiles to make disciples for me.

So having confined his own ministry to Israel, he is now sending Jews out into the world to make Gentiles into disciples of *Yeshua HaMashiach*. Thank God some of them did. Not all of them did, but some did. Thomas went to south India, and there are Indian Christians today who are the fruits of Thomas's going and making disciples of Gentiles. Peter went to Cornelius in Caesarea. Paul was the apostle to the Gentiles and he was the most Jewish Jew you could imagine. So thank God that some of the Jews who heard Jesus on that day did it.

But I have to say that most Jews today are not doing it. The calling of Israel from the beginning was to bless the whole world. Through Abraham, all the families of the earth will be blessed. From the very beginning, the calling of Israel was to be a light to the Gentiles, and in Isaiah chapter forty-three, in some older versions, it is said to Israel: *Ye are my witnesses, saith Jehovah.*

So Jews are called to be Jehovah's witnesses! Can you imagine what would happen if the young men of Israel were going round the world two by two, knocking on your door, saying we have come to tell you about the God of Israel? What a vision! What a possibility! That is their calling, and in Romans chapter eleven Paul says their gifts and their calling are irrevocable. That will never change. But sadly, the country of Israel has become a people primarily concerned with themselves, with their own safety, with their own security, with their own future, and many of the Israelis that I have talked to seem to have lost a sense of calling to be a light to us Gentiles, to show the world how blessed you can be when you live God's way. That is the tragedy of our day, and it grieves the God of Israel who called them to be missionaries, sent ones.

God still wants that nation to be a light to the Gentiles, and the good news is that one day they will fulfil their calling. One day, all Israel will be saved, and when they are, can you imagine what that will do for the whole world? *For if their rejection is the reconciliation of the world, what will their acceptance be but life from the dead?* (Romans 11:15, *NIV*). A resurrection of a nation, to fulfil its calling to the world. The whole world is going to be blessed when this nation again becomes what God meant it to be. And in those days, ten men will seize the clothes of one Jew and say, 'Tell me about your God.' It is going to happen, and so the Gospel of Matthew, that begins with the limited mission of Jesus to the lost sheep of the house of Israel, suddenly at the end broadens right out, when those five hundred Jews are told, *"Go and make disciples of all the Gentiles"*.

The New Testament is full of Israel. Do not stay in the Old. The Old is part of the Word of God, and a vital part, but the New completes it, and takes all the promises and sees them fulfilled in *Yeshua HaMashiach*.

2

ISRAEL IN ACTS

Dr Luke, from Antioch, companion to Paul in many of his travels, is the only Gentile author in the whole Bible. This is the second of his volumes, the first being his Gospel. He was a meticulous collector of facts, aiming at a thoroughly accurate account of the beginnings of this new faith. He has researched the life of its founder, a Jew called Jesus, and its chief purveyor, a Jew called Paul. It was all done for one man, Theophilus, possibly the Roman judge who would preside over Paul's trial and who would need a scrupulous presentation of all the relevant evidence. Luke's compilations, however, have had a much wider value for Christians through the ages, presenting as they do a unique portrait of Jesus as the Saviour of the world, and an illuminating insight into the life and growth of the early church.

Since most of the action in the book of Acts takes place in Gentile contexts, particularly in the second half, one might expect little to be said about Israel.

Nevertheless, there are some key statements relating to our theme of 'Israel in the New Testament'. We shall consider those made by Jesus himself, Peter, Stephen, James and Paul. The key question is whether the Jewish people have any future as a nation in God's plans or whether they have been left behind by the developing church.

1. WHAT JESUS SAID (1:6–8)

During the forty days between his resurrection from the dead and ascension into heaven, Jesus completed his training of the eleven remaining disciples to become his apostles. First, he convinced them he really was alive again with 'proofs' of visible and tangible appearances, even sharing meals with them. Second, he gave them further teaching about the kingdom of God. Third, he prepared them for his absence by promising a baptism of the Holy Spirit in the immediate future, for which they were to wait in Jerusalem before doing anything else.

But there was one notable omission. He said nothing about the future of his and their people, the nation of Israel. They were now convinced he was the promised Messiah, yet he had not fulfilled any of the prophetic predictions relating to a Davidic 'king of the Jews'. The nation was still under enemy occupation, ruled over by a Gentile Roman governor (Pilate) and an Edomite puppet king (Herod). Crowds had welcomed Jesus as their champion ('Hosanna' means 'Liberate us now') but were quickly disillusioned. The disciples might have shared their disappointment, but the resurrection had renewed their confidence and rekindled their hopes.

The burning question was blurted out at one of their last meals with Jesus. His answer to them has been the subject of controversy ever since, and Christians are still deeply divided over its significance for the people of Israel today.

THE QUESTION

So when they met together, they asked him, "Lord, are you at this time going to restore the kingdom to Israel?" (Acts 1:6, *NIV*.)

There is no dispute over what the disciples were asking. Every question is based on assumptions, which may or may not be correct. The classic example is: 'Have you stopped beating your wife?' This presupposes the husband has been doing so. A simple answer 'Yes' or 'No' would tacitly admit the charge. We shall return to this point when we consider Jesus' answer. Meanwhile, we need to analyse the question for its assumed conclusions, of which there were five:

(i) Israel used to be/have a 'kingdom'. That is, she had her own sovereign territory and political autonomy, ruled over by her own monarch and dynasty.

(ii) Israel has lost her 'kingdom'. For centuries she

has been a subject people, successively controlled by Egyptians, Syrians, Greeks and Romans.

(iii) The kingdom will be 'restored' to Israel. This expectation was based on prophetic promises of land and throne returned to them.

(iv) Jesus can restore the kingdom to Israel. They are now convinced about his divine person and power, so believe it is within his capability. 'Will *you* . . . ?'

(v) Jesus 'will' restore the kingdom to Israel. As the 'anointed one' (Messiah) he will fulfil all the predictions associated with his coming.

They are quite sure about all this and they expect Jesus to agree. The only uncertainty is the timing.

'At this time?' could simply be an alternative to 'Now?' or 'Soon?' But it may mean more than that. They know that Jesus will shortly be leaving them and returning to his heavenly home (see John 20:17) and that he would make a second 'coming' to the earth (they had already enquired about the signs of his approach and been told what they would be, Matthew 24:1–31.) So 'at *this* time?' may mean 'on this visit or at your second coming?' But we cannot be sure of that.

What we can be certain about is that they were not asking Jesus WHETHER he would restore the kingdom to Israel, but WHEN he would do so. And there can be no doubt they were thinking nationally, whether of their liberty, territory or monarchy — probably all three.

THE ANSWER

He said to them, "It is not for you to know the times or dates the Father has set by his own authority. But you will receive power when the Holy Spirit comes on you; and you will be my witnesses in Jerusalem, and in all Judea and Samaria, and to the ends of the earth" (Acts 1:7–8, *NIV*).

Jesus' reply is in two parts: a negative and a positive statement. It is the first that has caused controversy. There are two basic interpretations, completely contradictory to each other. Both have a profound effect on Christian attitudes to the Jewish people.

One interpretation claims that Jesus is not answering the question at all but dismissing it as mistaken, irrelevant and out of order. His evasive reply is intended to be a reproach for their obsolete thinking. After all his teaching on the kingdom of heaven for God, why are they still thinking of an earthly kingdom for Israel? All the presuppositions behind the question are wrong and need to be rebuked and corrected.

The positive part of his reply is then seen as rectifying their error. They should be thinking of a spiritual, not a political kingdom, a universal, not a national one, of which they were to be 'witnesses' to the whole human race. This mission may begin in the Jewish capital but must extend to the ends of the earth. This is what they should by now be thinking and asking about.

Though he has not directly answered their question

'When?', he has virtually said, 'Never.' Their agenda is not his. His 'answer' is deliberately intended to divert their attention from 'worldly' hopes to higher aspirations.

Not surprisingly, this approach is associated with 'replacement' theology, the idea that the church has replaced Israel as God's chosen people, making the latter redundant. But is it a sound exegesis of the text?

Look again at the first part of his answer. Consider first what is not there. No sign of impatience or even disappointment. No rebuke or reproach. No challenge, much less denial, of the presuppositions behind their question. Instead, he deals directly with the matter of timing, giving a straight but discouraging reply.

It is not for them to know when. Their curiosity will not be satisfied. They are obviously not in the 'need to know' circle. It is the privilege and responsibility of God the Father to 'set' the date. 'Times and seasons' are exclusively in his hands. Jesus is clearly saying that the decision is not within his own authority. He may even be implying that he does not know himself so could not tell them anyway. He confessed such ignorance on another occasion, then in relation to the timing of his second coming (Matthew 24:36). Is there a faint hint here that the restoration of the kingdom to Israel is linked to his return, the timing of both unknown to anyone else save the Father only? See below on Acts 3:21.

That last thought may be sheer speculation, but what is absolutely certain is that Jesus has *not* denied the validity of their enquiry. He has tacitly accepted their expectation as part of God's intended plans. He has allowed them to go on hoping that one day it will happen, even if they remain ignorant of the timing. Whereas in much human conversation 'God only knows' is a colloquial expression of doubt as to whether something will ever happen, on Jesus' lips it is an affirmation of confidence that he will bring it about in his own good time.

So to the question 'When?', Jesus' answer means, 'I won't tell you', or even, 'I can't tell you.' But that is a world away from saying, 'Never.' It is more like, 'Sometime.' He has the ability to do it, but not the authority to decide when to do it.

One indication that this is the better interpretation is that the disciples accepted his answer without any discussion, much less any protest or argument. They were content to leave it to his Father to decide when.

The second, more positive, part of the answer takes on a rather different flavour. The international mission is not the correct alternative to a national restoration, but the more immediate task to be fulfilled beforehand. Not 'instead' but 'meanwhile'. There is something else to be done first (cf. Romans 11:25–26, which we shall look at in the next chapter). The rest of the book of Acts shows that they got on and did it.

2. WHAT PETER SAID (3:12–26)

The beggar who asked for alms was given legs instead! Lame from birth, he was carried to the temple gate every day, so that his disability might touch the generosity of worshippers. It is a situation common to many cultures and countries. Peter had no wealth, but he could contribute health — in the powerful name of Jesus. However, it not only meant the cripple could walk; he would now have to work as well! When the people saw this familiar figure literally dancing for joy, a curious and astonished crowd quickly gathered, giving Peter an audience for his second public preaching.

As we study his speech, we will stand amazed at the radical change in this one-time fisherman. Just weeks earlier he had been so fearful that he denied any connection with Jesus, three times and to a little girl, though she was a servant in the high priest's house and might have reported him to her employer; and there were others listening to the exchange.

Now he would openly risk his life by publicly accusing those responsible in any way, direct or indirect, for the murder of his friend Jesus. What explains this radical change from cowardice to courage? He had been baptised in the Holy Spirit during the Jewish feast of Pentecost. This gave him the two gifts of 'tongues' (Greek: *glossai*) to speak to God more effectively, and 'boldness' (Greek: *paresia*) to speak to men more effectively. Would that all who desire the former would also want the latter!

INDICTMENT

Peter began with a brief explanation of how the miracle had been done. It was not that they (John had been there too) had any special powers or were unusually pious. It was the power of the God of Israel, the God of the nation's fathers, released through Jesus, whom he had now 'glorified', the divine reversal of the verdict that had led to his execution.

Peter then proceeded to charge all his hearers with what was in God's eyes the murder of an innocent person! It is certain that none of them had taken part in the crucifixion itself. That was the work of Gentile Roman soldiers. Nor would they have been members of the Sanhedrin, the court that tried and condemned him. Nor could many of them have been part of the crowd in Pilate's small courtyard, who had demanded death on a cross. More could have watched him carry the means of his death on the painful road to the place of execution, now called the Via Dolorosa, the way of sorrows. Some may have joined in the mocking ridicule as he hung naked, bleeding and dying. But the fact remains that of the thousands who had greeted him as a hero just days before, not one raised a finger to save him or even protested at what was the greatest ever miscarriage of justice. They were all 'accessories after the fact'. They had simply let it happen.

Peter does not spare his listeners. Looking them in the eye, he accuses them with an emphatic second person plural pronoun: YOU handed him over to be killed. YOU disowned him before Pilate. YOU disowned the Holy and Righteous One and called for a murderer to be released. YOU killed the author of life. He obviously believed in the concept of personal and corporate guilt. 'You' means 'all of you'.

The atmosphere is that of a courtroom. Peter is the self-appointed counsel for the prosecution. Peter and John are both 'witnesses' of the crime but primarily of the divine vindication of the victim by raising him from the dead. Then Peter becomes counsel for the defence and pleads the mitigating circumstances of ignorance. They had simply not realised what they were doing (an echo of Jesus' own prayer on the cross, Luke 23:34). However, ignorance is not innocence. Sin is still sin, whether we know we are committing it or not. However, the guilt is greater when we know full well that what we are doing is wrong. Peter as the judge has found them all guilty.

This is not the first time Peter has dared to say such things. In his very first 'sermon' on the day of Pentecost itself, he had concluded with, *"Therefore, let **all Israel** be assured of this: God has made this Jesus, whom YOU crucified both Lord and Christ"* [Messiah] (Acts 2:36, my emphasis). Nor would it be the last time. Arrested after his second speech, he and John were hauled before the very same leaders who had tried and condemned Jesus. Defending the healing miracle performed on the crippled beggar, Peter said, *"Know this, YOU and **everyone else in Israel**: It is by the name of Jesus Christ of Nazareth, whom YOU crucified but whom God raised from the dead, that this man stands before you healed"* (4:10, my emphasis). No wonder his hearers were impressed with his courage.

INSTRUCTION

All was not lost, however. The guilty need not be condemned and punished, as their victim had been. There was hope for them. They could avoid being accused by God when all will have to stand before him. And this in spite of the fact that they had murdered the 'Holy and Righteous One' sent by God himself for their benefit.

Only God could let them off such a crime against himself. But there was a necessary condition — repentance. This is a change in thought, word and deed. It would involve changing their minds about Jesus and their verdict on him, confessing their sin and guilt in letting him die, and joining those who believed in and were following him, including being baptised in his name. On the first occasion we know that three thousand seized the opportunity and were baptised. On the third occasion, the apostles were arrested, later released but forbidden to talk about Jesus in public again. When they did so, and they were re-arrested and appeared before the Sanhedrin, the very body that had condemned Jesus to die, they met with angry resentment. *"You . . . are determined to make us guilty of this man's blood"* (5:28).

On this second occasion, which we are looking at in more detail, there is no record of any response from the crowd that had gathered in the temple. Actually, the apostles were arrested before they had finished speaking. But it may be that Peter sensed that he was not seeing any signs of conviction of sin, as at Pentecost, for he added both strong incentives and a severe warning to his appeal for repentance.

The warning related to a prediction of Moses that God would send a prophet like himself (who delivered the nation from bondage). The penalty for not 'listening' to him, which includes doing what he said, would be to be *completely cut off from their people* (see Deuteronomy 18:15–19). That rescuer had been and gone, but they could still listen, or else . . . .

INCENTIVE

Peter promised four wonderful results if they turned to the Lord in true repentance.

First, there would be remission of their sins. They would literally be excised from the record, wiped out, scraped off, (the same word is used as of names 'blotted out' from the book of life in Revelation 3:5). They would be as if they had never been committed. God could declare them innocent (the legal meaning of 'justification'). They could be acquitted and leave the court as free.

But forgiveness is not just being let off. It is much more than that. It is the restoration of a relationship with the one who has been hurt and wronged. Israel could be reconciled with their God, who could have punished them for what they had done to the 'Holy and Righteous One' he had sent for them. It was an amazing offer.

Second, they would have rest from their enemies. The phrase 'seasons of refreshing' has recently been so over-used to describe bursts of intense spiritual enthusiasm such as have happened in church history, especially in the eighteenth and nineteenth centuries, that it is difficult to imagine what the words would mean to Peter's Jewish hearers. If the Old Testament is any guide, the phrase would convey the idea of periods of peace, no longer under enemy attack, times when they did not need to fear invasion, occupation or even deportation. A time of rest, recovery, recuperation when things could return to normal and life could be lived as it should.

Of course, the spiritual aspect would be included, but that would not be exclusive to other needs — physical, for example. And there would be national implications, as Peter went on to mention.

Third, the return of their Messiah. The little word 'that', in "... *that he may send the Messiah*" (3:20), indicates a link between the condition of Israel as a people and Jesus' return to earth. They had not been ready for his first visit but need to be for his second. He was coming back to the same place and the same people, though his purpose both times was for all peoples the world over.

Peter also emphasised Jesus' strong connection with Israel. He was, *". . . the Messiah, who has been appointed for you"* (3:20). This ties in with the words of Jesus, *"I was sent only to the lost sheep of Israel"* (Matthew 15:24, *NIV*).

Fourth, restoration of their past. With this prophecy we come to the most important statement in Peter's speech for the purpose of this book, because of its bearing on the fundamental issue of whether the nation of Israel has a future in God's plan and purpose.

He is absolutely certain that a time will come when God will restore 'everything'. The word 'restore' means to return anything to its former condition. But what does 'everything' cover? Peter qualifies this to mean everything that God has promised through the prophets. God always keeps his word, however 'long ago' he said it.

These divine pledges certainly had a *universal* aspect. God had told Isaiah that he intended to create a new heaven [space] and earth [our planet] (Isaiah 66:22.)

But most of the predictions about God's future

activities were *national*. It would be difficult, if not impossible, for Peter's Jewish audience to think otherwise. Israel's return to the land and the Lord, under a Davidic king, bringing lasting peace and prosperity, were repeated by so many prophets in the *Tanach* (Jewish scriptures, our 'Old Testament') that it would be an act of vandalism to cut them out.

It is very significant that Peter uses the same word for 'restore' as was used of the question he and other disciples had asked about Jesus 'restoring' the kingdom to Israel (Acts 1:6). He is now clearly convinced it will happen, after the Messiah returns.

Those who believe that the church has 'replaced' or 'fulfilled' Israel tell us that such promises are 'not to be taken literally'! Why not? Who says so? By what principle of interpretation? Is it not a Protestant Reformation axiom that scripture must be accepted in its plainest, simplest sense unless there is a clear reason in the text or context for taking it otherwise?

The prophecies relating to the first coming of the Messiah were fulfilled literally. Why should those relating to his second be any different? The statistics of our Bible as an almanac of the future are impressive. Of the 735 separate events predicted in its pages (24% of its verses include one), 596 have come to pass — literally. That is over 80%. It does not require much faith to believe that the remainder will also happen, equally literally.

Should not Peter, as a 'Christian' and part of the 'church', have told his hearers that God's promises to the prophets of long ago must not be taken literally but were all 'metaphorical' and must be applied 'spiritually' to the new people of God? Should he not have been more careful not to raise false hopes? Such thinking seems ludicrous to common sense. Enough said.

Quite simply, Peter was expressing his complete confidence that whatever God has promised to do he will do, however long we may have to wait for it. He was speaking as a Jew and a believer in Jesus (he would not have called himself a 'Christian'; that was a nickname for Gentile disciples, Acts 11:26). His hearers would have taken him at his word, quite literally. He meant them to.

3. WHAT STEPHEN SAID (7:1–53)

Surprisingly, Stephen said more about Israel in this book of Acts than anyone else. Indeed, his is the longest discourse recorded here. But it is mostly about Israel's past, partly about her present and nothing at all about her future. Even so, it led directly to his death as the first of many Christian martyrs.

THE SITUATION

Some facts need to be mentioned. First, there were two kinds of Jews in the early church: the Hebraic (born and bred in Israel, with Hebrew language and culture) and the Hellenistic (who had lived in the Diaspora with Greek language and culture). Separate synagogues in Jerusalem allowed for their different backgrounds. Second, the early church had a welfare programme for the needy, particularly for widows who had lost their only means of support.

Complaints arose among the 'Greek' widows that the distributors of food were unfair, giving more to the 'Hebrew'. The apostles were notified and took immediate steps to put things right. Declining to be distracted from their own vital ministry of teaching and preaching, they suggested choosing a team of seven to oversee the catering programme. It is intriguing that they stipulated men rather than women, and even more interesting that for a mundane, even menial, task of waiting on tables, they demanded high spiritual qualifications: 'full of the Holy Spirit and wisdom' (they would certainly need the latter). Some see this incident as the foundation of the later office of 'deacon', which means 'servant'. They were set apart with prayer and laying on of hands for this domestic task.

Thus was Stephen brought to wider notice, the first chosen by popular acclaim. He quickly became known for miraculous signs as well as mundane service, for he was also *full of God's grace **and power***. For some reason, which we are not told, this aroused intense hostility in a 'Greek' synagogue. They could not stand Stephen's deeds and they could not match his words. So they persuaded some men to tell lies about his preaching, accusing him of blasphemy against God and Moses, against the temple and the law (note the similarity to the charges brought against Jesus). Reported to the authorities, he was brought to trial before Israel's governing body, the Sanhedrin (the very council which had found Jesus guilty of blasphemy).

His judges were rivetted by his appearance, his face shining as if reflecting supernatural glory. Then he was given an opportunity to defend himself. As we shall see, he never even tried to. Far from denying the charges, he turned the tables by accusing his judges of committing a far more serious crime. But he took rather a long time to get round to that!

THE SPEECH

It is an extraordinary statement, a cross between a lecture and a sermon. Not once did Stephen mention himself or his supposed crimes. Instead, he gave them a potted history of the nation of Israel, with which his audience would already be more than familiar. They must have been surprised and puzzled by such an unexpected response. But they could not help but go on looking and listening. What on earth was he getting at? The answer was them! Yet it would be some time before they realised that.

His survey of the past focussed on some of their great heroes: Abraham, Joseph, Moses, David and

Solomon. These were great men of God who had played a major role in the foundation, preservation, liberation and institution of their nation, culminating in its greatest expansion. Behind all of them were the covenantal promises and providence of God, revealing himself in words and deeds. No other nation had such a unique history.

Why would Stephen remind them of it? Like all history, especially a brief overview of nearly two millennia, a careful and meaningful selection of events has to be made. This is done in accordance with the historian's purpose of discerning a pattern and deriving a lesson. Thus, history can have a message, an example, for later generations. Running through Stephen's summary are two relevant themes, one minor and the other major.

The minor point concerns the temple in Jerusalem. He had been accused of publicising Jesus of Nazareth's threat to 'destroy this place', where the Sanhedrin was meeting. Actually Jesus had been referring to his own body as the temple of God on earth, promising to raise it up again in three days (Matthew 26:61).

Stephen was pointing out that most of God's significant interventions in their history had not taken place in the temple at all, or even in the promised land. He is not bound to any particular place. He had for the most part lived in a tent, a mobile dwelling place. When David wanted to erect a permanent building for

God, feeling embarrassed that he had built a palace
for himself, he was rebuked for thinking God needed
or even wanted it. After it was built, by David's son
Solomon, the prophet Isaiah pointed out that the
Creator and sustainer of the entire universe is hardly
likely to be confined to a building made by human
hands. So Stephen seems to be telling his accusers they
have an inflated idea of their temple's importance.

The major point of his address, however, concerns
their attitude revealed in the way they have reacted
to God's servants sent to help them. The nation has a
consistent history of rejecting them. Joseph was sold
into slavery by his own brothers, though he would
be their saviour in famine. No sooner had Moses got
them out of Egypt than they rebelled against him
and his God, asking his brother Aaron to lead them
into idolatry and immorality. Though God gave them
ground rules to make possible a happy, healthy and holy
community life, they continually disobeyed them. The
Old Testament is the history of a stiff-necked, stubborn
people, whose proud independence constantly tested
God's patience. In passing we may notice that every
appeal to the example of Israel in the New Testament
is essentially negative: don't do what they did.

At one point there is a dramatic change in Stephen's
speech. It becomes more heated, much more personal
(note the introduction of 'you'). The accused becomes
the accuser. He has literally turned on his judges,

charging them with being no better and even worse than their ancestors. They had persecuted the prophets, but *"now you have betrayed and murdered the Righteous One"* (the promised anointed king).

All this echoes the parable of the wicked tenants who had abused the servants of the vineyard owner and finally killed his son (Matthew 21:33–46). But this time the message was being spelled out in historical fact rather than literary fiction. However, the effect on the hearers was the same — to stir up their hatred.

THE SEQUEL

His audience were furious with what they took to be offensive insults and gnashed their teeth, a threatening gesture seen more often in animals. But Stephen hardly noticed. He was looking up, right into heaven, and saw the Son of Man at God's right hand (another echo of Jesus' trial, Mark 14:62). He told the Sanhedrin what he could see and this only enraged them further, confirming the charge of blasphemy. They clapped their hands to their eyes and yelled to drown out any further words, and dragged him out of the city to stone him to death. This was indeed the Mosaic penalty for blasphemy, but they seem to have been so angry that they temporarily forgot that the Romans had forbidden them to use capital punishment themselves, as had happened on another occasion in connection with Jesus himself (John 8:59).

There were more than echoes of Jesus' death in Stephen's two final words as he died, though in reverse order. He committed his spirit to the Lord as his body perished (though to Jesus rather than to the Father) and he prayed for the forgiveness of his executioners. A truly Christian death of the first martyr.

To summarise this whole tragic episode, Stephen's account of Israel is the most pessimistic in the whole book of Acts. Not once does he offer any hope of change in the national character. He neither urges them to repentance nor offers them forgiveness as Peter had done. If this was the last word about the Jewish people, it would be tempting to write them off as beyond redemption. But it is not God's last word, as we shall see in the next chapter.

4. WHAT JAMES SAID (15:16–17)

The apostle James said nothing about the nation of Israel as such, but on one crucial occasion he mentioned the *rebuilding of David's fallen tent*, a clear reference to the former king of Israel and the restoration of something connected with his reign, a thousand years before. James was quoting a promise made through the prophet Amos a couple of centuries after David and eight before James. So what did 'fallen tent' mean? Why did Amos and James use the phrase?

The words only occur twice in the whole Bible, once in the Old Testament and once in the New, and the latter is a quotation of the former. We should be careful, therefore, not to build too much on such a flimsy foundation. For such a rare text, context is very important. There are three contexts to be considered, those of David, Amos and James.

There were many 'tents' in David's day. He lived in one during his rise to power. After assembling with him from time to time, the people left, 'each to his own tent', so most of them were still living in tents. After conquering Jerusalem, David then built a palace for himself (its ruins have only recently been unearthed by young archaeologists, south of the Temple Mount); but this made David feel guilty because the Lord's presence was still represented by a tent, the mobile 'tabernacle' (same word) erected by Moses during forty years in the wilderness and now standing in Gibeon where daily sacrifices were offered. However, when the kidnapped ark from the Holy of holies was recovered from the Philistines, David did not return it to the tabernacle in Gibeon but put up another tent for it in Jerusalem, where worship and sacrifice were offered. Strictly speaking, only this one qualified for the description 'David's tent'.

But is this what the prophecy of Amos was referring to? Look at his context. He was not a prophet at all, but a small farmer in Tekoa, a hamlet in the south of Israel. A civil war had followed the death of Solomon and the ten tribes in the north had split from the two in the south (big Judah and little Benjamin). Claiming the name 'Israel' as the majority, they had their own monarch and temple. Their rebellious pride quickly led to corruption in religion and ethics, idolatry and immorality. Inevitably, social injustice was rife.

Amos was sent to warn them about the inevitable consequences if such a state of affairs continued. They would forfeit their right to stay in the promised land. It must have taken considerable courage for a southerner to deliver such a damning indictment to the northerners. Their response could well have been: 'Who do you think you are, telling us what to do?'

However, though most Old Testament prophets are known for their 'doom and gloom' predictions, their pessimism about the immediate future was usually balanced with optimism about the ultimate future. The clouds of despair had a silver lining of hope. Amos ends his denunciation with prospects of restored fertility, prosperity, and above all, the return of the people to 'their own land, never again to be uprooted'.

It is in this context that God promises to restore David's tent, repairing its broken walls and rebuilding its ruins. The language makes it unlikely that 'tent' was ever intended to be taken literally. A structure of poles, cloth, ropes and pegs would hardly fall into ruins with broken walls and would be 'pitched' or re-erected rather than rebuilt. It suggests that 'tent' is a figure of speech, a metaphor for something else.

In passing we may note that God himself will do this. The prophecy begins with the emphatic, *"I will"* and ends with: *". . . declares the Lord, who will do these things."* By contrast, *"they"* (the returning Israelites) *"will rebuild the ruined cities"*.

In the middle of all this (Amos 9:11–12) is a striking reference to possessing 'the remnant of Edom', a major antagonist of Israel right back to their forty-year journey to the promised land, as well as, *"all the nations that bear my name"*. So non-Israelites, Gentiles, will be included when David's tent is restored.

This last aspect is undoubtedly the reason why James remembered and repeated these verses centuries later, after Jesus had been and gone. His context was the first general council of the Christian church (recorded in Acts 15). Apostles and elders had met in Jerusalem to consider a crisis that could have split the early church.

The first members were all Jewish, as were the twelve apostles and Jesus himself — or at least Jewish proselytes already attached to Jewish synagogues. But now Peter and Paul were introducing Gentile outsiders to Christian faith and fellowship. The question was bound to arise: should Gentiles who wanted to follow the Jewish Messiah become good Jews first? The issue focussed in the iniatory rite of circumcision, carrying with it the obligation to live by all the laws revealed to Moses. Opinion was sharply divided. There were

'Judaising' believers who would follow Paul around trying to persuade his converts to be circumcised (read his letter to the Galatians for a strong rebuttal). Incidentally, there is a contemporary parallel opposite to this, namely: Does a Jew believing in Jesus have to become like Gentiles and leave Jewish identity behind? Perhaps the earlier crisis provides guidelines to deal with the modern dilemma.

How did they settle the issue then? They did not take a vote on opinions, which could be very subjective. They looked for objective evidence in the shape of the Spirit's deeds and the scripture's words, a decisive combination.

The Lord had clearly poured out his Spirit on Gentiles, as Peter and Paul could both testify. This was a 'seal' of his acceptance of them into his family, their adoption as sons. How could Jewish believers insist on further qualifications?

However, it is significant that further confirmation was also sought in scripture, which at that stage meant the Jewish 'canon', our Old Testament. James could have chosen from a number of prophecies that Gentile nations were included in God's future plans. (Paul would later select Hosea 2:23 and 1:10; see Romans 9:25–26). James chose Amos (9:11–12), a prophet who had preceded Hosea among the ten northern tribes.

James' quotation does not exactly match the original prophecy. For one thing he seems to be quoting from the later Greek translation of the Hebrew (called the 'Septuagint' or 'LXX' for short, because seventy scholars had worked on it). He adds words, like 'I will return' at the beginning, and omits others, like the reference to 'Edom'. He may even be incorporating allusions to other prophecies, like Jeremiah 12:15 and Isaiah 45:21. But the gist of his quotation is quite clear. The prophets had foretold an influx of Gentile nations into the people and 'this is that' which the early church was now witnessing. It was all in line with the word of God.

James gave his 'judgement' that Gentiles need not become Jews to belong to God's people. Circumcision and observing all the Mosaic laws were not essential qualifications. However, there remained the practical problem of holding the two cultures together in one community. So for the sake of fellowship Gentile believers were advised to respect the scruples of Jewish believers, in matters of diet, for example (verse 29).

So far, so good. But, as we have noted, James had included in his quotation a reference to a rebuilding of David's tent (Amos 9:11) as well as the inclusion of the Gentiles (Amos 9:12). Was this deliberate or simply due to the fact that verses 11 and 12 form one sentence and James was using the whole statement for the sake of its second half only? Certainly, the implication in Amos is that the rebuilding of David's tent and the Gentile influx are directly related, the latter being the consequence of the former (note the phrase 'so that', joining the two predictions). We may therefore assume that James is also drawing attention to the connection.

We are left with two vital questions: what and when? What is the meaning of David's tent? When will it be 'rebuilt'? There are three different answers to both questions and we have to decide between them.

So what does the tent signify or symbolise? No-one takes it literally. To do so would mean that God himself would one day erect a structure of poles, cloth, ropes and stakes. So all interpreters take 'tent' metaphorically, but in three different ways.

(i) THE DAVIDIC GOVERNMENT

In any nomadic people, the chief's tent is the seat of government, his 'throne-room' in which all decisions are made and from which all decrees are issued. It is the seat of his authority.

It is therefore understood that David's tent would be restored when the promised 'son of David' was enthroned.

The majority of Christian commentators assume that this has already happened, when Jesus, one of whose titles is 'Son of David' ascended to heaven for his coronation and enthronement. He is now sharing with his Father the throne of the universe, all authority in heaven and on earth delegated to him (Matthew 28:18).

Some emphasise his reign over the whole earth, over all nations, Jewish and Gentile, while admitting that not all his enemies are as yet under his feet. Others focus on his rule over those clearly submitted to his lordship, that is, the church. Whatever, he is now reigning on high, indirectly over the world and directly over the church. David's tent/throne has been rebuilt.

Going back to James, it is assumed that he, too, saw it as an event in the (near) past. The influx of Gentile believers is then seen not just as a consequence but also as a proof that the predictions of Amos were then being fulfilled. 'David's tent' was future in the Old Testament but past in the New.

Such an interpretation fits well into 'replacement' theology, which has a practice of 'spiritualising' predictions about Israel and applying them to the church. In this case, 'David's tent' has been replaced with something far bigger and better.

But something very different! David's government was based down on earth; this one is up in heaven. David's was national, this is international. Are the two sufficiently comparable to be described by the same title? Does the present situation really fulfil the many promises that Israel will one day have its own monarchy as well as its own territory? These can be derisively dismissed as belonging to the Old Testament and 'not to be taken literally'. But there are such predictions in the New Testament as well. Take two examples:

> *"The Lord God will give him* [Mary's son, Jesus] *the throne of his father David, and he will reign over the house of Jacob for ever, his kingdom will never end"* (Luke 1:32–33, spoken by the angel Gabriel; did he get it wrong?)

> *"Truly I tell you, at the renewal of all things, when the Son of Man sits on his glorious throne, you who have followed me will sit on twelve thrones, judging the twelve tribes of Israel"* (Matthew 19:28, spoken by Jesus himself; would he mislead them?)

It is patently obvious that none of this has happened yet. Half the Jews are back in the promised land, but 'Israel' is a democracy as decadent as any in the Western world, hardly a restoration of David's kingdom. We must therefore consider other interpretations.

(ii) THE DAVIDIC WORSHIP

This was a novel interpretation which surfaced some forty years ago, when Pentecostal phenomena appeared in mainline denominations. Building on the King James (Authorised) version's translation of 'tent' as 'tabernacle' (actually the same word), it was taken as a religious structure and presumed to refer to the tent which David erected in Jerusalem to house the recovered ark of the covenant (1 Chronicles 16:1). The rest of the chapter describes in detail the praise offered at the event, accompanied by musical instruments. David ordered this ministry to continue daily, as well as the daily sacrifice at Moses' tabernacle, still standing in Gibeon.

How did this come to be associated with the 'charismatic renewal' in the second half of the twentieth century? Every rediscovery of the Holy Spirit's power and presence in the history of the church has found an expression in singing new songs to the Lord. The most notable example is the eighteenth century revival, when John and Charles Wesley between them wrote over six thousand new hymns packed with biblical allusions. The same thing happened in the 1960s and 1970s. A couple in New Zealand published a book entitled *Scripture in Song*. These 'choruses', as they came to be known, were shorter than traditional hymns, often consecutive Bible verses set to contemporary music. There was to be a worldwide explosion of such new songs, assisted by technological developments in amplification and communication. The book of Psalms proved a rich mine for new material, fostering an affinity with King David. Other aspects of the worship he led became widely accepted practice. Bodily actions such as uplifted arms, clapping hands and dancing feet were now seen in many churches. To guitars were added a variety of other instruments, and waving banners followed.

I have not been able to track down who, but someone read about 'David's tabernacle restored' in either Acts or Amos, or both, and leapt to the conclusion that this described what was happening. With the speed of modern communication, both the idea and the phrase caught on, and became the label for the ascendancy of music in worship. Indeed, the outward aspect of corporate worship came to be defined in terms of music, almost exclusively. Announcing a time of worship often meant handing over leadership to the musicians. No longer was the reading or preaching considered to be part of worship. (I have often been told, 'We'll be having a time of worship before/after you preach.') Prayer, especially intercession, was often reduced to a minimum. Even prayer would often be accompanied by music, to make it more 'worshipful'. The Lord's Supper could seem almost an anti-climax after the singing, clapping and dancing.

So there was a radical change in many weekly Sunday services. Historically, the traditional pattern in many denominations had been largely based on synagogue worship — combining praise, preaching and prayer — in which systematic reading of scripture played a prominent role. Now the celebrations in the temple (annual, for obvious practical reasons), in which the Word played less part, became regarded as normative by many. Once this major development was linked with the restoration of David's tabernacle, Christian musicians had the extra motivation of believing they were actually fulfilling ancient prophecy in their own generation. This consciousness of being agents bringing God's Word to pass was incorporated in songs. One well-known chorus spoke of these being the days of David, and of 'rebuilding the temple of praise'. Actually, David did not build the temple. He had blood on his hands so he was disqualified and had to leave the task to his son Solomon, though he did collect the required materials.

But is this identification with Davidic worship valid? And is the prediction by Amos at last being fulfilled in this generation? Are we the privileged people able to say, 'This is that which was spoken by the prophet Amos'? There is at least one telling reason why the 'tent' may not represent Davidic worship: simply, that it had not 'fallen into ruins' by the time of Amos. The temple was still standing in Jerusalem. Its choirs and orchestras were still intact. The annual festivals were still being held. The pilgrims were still singing. Yet Amos talks as if David's 'tent' was already a thing of the past. We must consider a third possible meaning.

(iii) THE DAVIDIC EMPIRE

How could a 'tent' resemble an empire? We tend to think of tents in a limited fashion, holding a small number of people in rather cramped conditions, reserving the word 'marquee' for larger structures. We have to revise this thinking when we first catch sight of a Bedouin encampment. Their sprawling tents have a number of 'rooms', for men, women and children, and are easily expanded to accommodate an extended family, many relatives and ever-welcome visitors.

It is a fitting metaphor for the increasing territory ruled over by David. During his reign the borders expanded to the south, east and north (the Mediterranean Sea lay to the west). Furthermore, he had taken in a number of Gentile nations, including Philistia, Amalek, Moab, Ammon, Syria, Zobah and, above all, one of their ancient foes, Edom. He had gained most of the land promised by God, to the southern border of the River (or brook) of Egypt, a prominent *wadi* just below what is now called the Gaza strip. He had not quite reached the Euphrates river in the north, but Solomon completed that by conquering Hamath. It was the nearest Israel ever came to being an imperial power, David's 'tent' covering most of this vital territory linking Europe, Asia and Africa. It had taken a millennium to build it up but it would all disappear in much less than that.

It had certainly 'fallen' by the time of Amos. After

Solomon, the civil war had taken ten of the twelve tribes out from under the Davidic dynasty. The weakened centre quickly lost control of the other nations on the circumference. David's empire had collapsed and would disappear altogether after the ten tribes in the north were invaded by Assyria and the two tribes in the south were deported to Babylon. Even the minority who managed to return never regained their secure political autonomy with their own monarch, except for a brief interlude during the Maccabean revolt, quickly followed by the Roman occupation.

If this is what 'David's tent' means, then it is quite clear that it has not yet been 'rebuilt'. Both the prediction of Amos and James' quotation await fulfilment in the future, unlike the 'Davidic government', which has already been fulfilled in the past and 'Davidic worship', which is being fulfilled in the present.

So when will it happen? We have already noted some hints in this book of Acts. There was the possibility that the kingdom would be restored to Israel 'the next time' Jesus came to earth (see our comments on Jesus' reply to the disciples' question in 1:6–7). Peter linked with his second coming the time for God to 'restore' (same word as in 1:6) everything, *"as he promised long ago through his holy prophets"* (3:21, which must surely include Amos).

It may be significant that James added an extra phrase to the beginning of his quotation from Amos, namely, *"After this **I will return** and rebuild David's tent . . . ."*

We conclude that the prophecy of Amos will be fulfilled when Jesus comes back to earth. This assumes he is coming back to reign over this world for an extended period (the premillennial view in eschatology), that one day, *"The kingdom of the world has become the kingdom of our Lord and of his Messiah"* (Revelation 11:15). The Davidic empire will be rebuilt, with the restored kingdom of Israel at its core and 'all the nations' (Amos), 'the rest of humanity' (James) within its compass. This empire of the Son of David will, of course, be on a grander scale than the earlier one, but the basic structure will be identical, with the Jerusalem throne at its centre.

Preparations for its rebuilding have been going on for two thousand years. Millions of Gentiles are being groomed for citizenship. Now Jews are turning to their Messiah more than ever before. And one day, when enough Gentiles are ready, 'all Israel' will submit to her King (see our study of Romans 11:25–26 in the next chapter). This reverse order has been a surprise but is part of God's wise plan.

Can we say anything positive about the two inter-pretations of 'David's tent' we have rejected (i.e. government and worship), apart from their claim to fulfilment in the past or present? Yes, we can; and both the influx of Gentiles in James' day and the explosion of musical celebration in our own day can be seen as *foretastes* of the final fulfilment — but not the fulfilment itself. It is the besetting temptation of each generation of biblical Christians, especially those with an excessive interest in 'end-time' prophecy, to mistake foretastes for fulfilment, indentifying current events with ancient predictions. For example, the apostle John wrote that '*many* antichrists' will be seen before '*the* Antichrist' appears (1 John 2:18). Yet each of the many has been thought to be the final one. (Luther thought it was the pope, and he returned the compliment; other candidates were Napoleon, Hitler and Stalin, as well as more recent political figures.) Each identification has led to speculation about the imminent return of our Lord, with dating quickly disproved.

Mistaking foretastes for fulfilment is rife in Christian Zionism. The establishment of the State of Israel in 1948 was an amazing foretaste of, and vital step towards, the final fulfilment when *all* the Jews will be brought back from the four corners of the earth —only about half so far. The retaking of Jerusalem in 1967 was a striking foretaste of the completion of 'the times of the Gentiles' (Luke 21:24) but not the end itself. Prophecies about an international assault on the capital have yet to be fulfilled (Zechariah 12:1–2 and 14:1–2).

The pressure and speed of world events can easily make us feel that we are in the very 'last days', that we are the final generation, who will experience the end of the age. But scripture exhorts us to remain awake and sober (1 Thessalonians 5:6) watching for the signs Jesus himself gave us. Of the four 'signals' he gave (in Matthew 24), not even two have been completed yet.

As a final example of mistaken identity, the destruction of the Twin Towers of the World Trade Center in New York was not the fulfilment of the fall of Babylon (in Revelation 18, particularly verses 17–19), though at the time many asked me if it was. But it was a vivid foretaste, a remarkable foreshadowing.

I know it is exciting to think that we are witnessing the fulfilment of old prophecies in our own day, before our very eyes. And I do believe we are seeing the beginning of the end, though we have been living in the 'last days' since the Holy Spirit was first poured out at Pentecost (Acts 2:17). But we need to remember that there is a task to be completed before the end can come. It is the Lord's desire and intention to have in his kingdom members of every tribe and language and people and nation (Revelation 5:9). Therefore, "...this gospel of the kingdom will be preached in the whole world as a testimony to all nations, and then the end will come" (Matthew 24:14, NIV).

5. WHAT PAUL SAID (28:17–27)

This book has been misnamed 'the Acts of the Apostles'. While two of the twelve, Peter and John, are prominent in the first few chapters, the rest are hardly mentioned, and most of the other chapters are about Paul, not even one of the Twelve.

This fits in with the hypothesis that Paul's friend, Dr Luke, from Antioch and probably a Gentile, wrote it in anticipation of Paul's trial in Rome. It was written for one man, Theophilus, who is given the title of a Roman judge or leading lawyer. This would explain why so much space is given to the last of Paul's numerous shipwrecks, in which he saved the lives of his Roman guards and voluntarily came on to Rome with them, when he could so easily have escaped. It also explains why there are such full accounts of his earlier trials, all of which found him innocent; and why the book closes abruptly with Paul under house arrest awaiting a summons to Caesar's court.

This last situation was the context for his last speech on record, which we have selected for a study of his thoughts on his own nation of Israel. He was still relatively free to address whoever he chose, but they would have to come to him rather than he to them. Within three days of his arrival in Rome he invited the leaders of the Jewish community in the metropolis to meet with him.

It was his consistent custom in every new place

to begin his mission among his fellow-Jews. He had been converted on Gentile soil (near Damascus) and called to be an apostle to the Gentile people (Acts 9:3 and 26:16–18). Why then did he always go to the Jews first? Well, they already believed in the same God as he did. Their scriptures and national history had already prepared them to receive the gospel. Jesus was their Messiah. They were already well on the way to accepting and following him. Above all, he felt indebted to them for all they had given him and believed they had the right to have the first opportunity to hear the good news of salvation.

Yet the Jewish response had been mixed, even meagre, and he had more than once found that non-Jews, Gentiles, were more eager to hear what he had to say. So he had quickly left the Jews and 'turned to the Gentiles' (Acts 13:46 and 18:6). Now in Rome it would happen again.

At his first meeting with them he explained how he came to be in his present situation, assuring them he had "... *done nothing against our people or against the customs of our ancestors ...*" (28:17). However, Jews had arrested him and handed him over to the Romans (echoes of Jesus!). To gain a fair trial he had exercised his right as a Roman citizen and appealed to Caesar. His 'crime' is to believe in 'the hope of Israel', almost certainly referring to their expectation of the coming Messiah, though Paul is not more explicit at this meeting.

They tell him they have not heard anything detrimental about himself personally, but they have certainly picked up the gossip about this new movement among Jewish people, which they had regarded as a 'sect', a variation within the Jewish faith rather than a departure from it. Paul had aroused their curiosity, so that 'larger numbers' came to hear him on a second visit.

This time Paul kept them for a whole day. Taking as his theme the kingdom of God, he took them through their own scriptures, to persuade them that Jesus was their Messiah. Some were convinced, but others refused to believe it. The group began to break up in heated arguments with each other. Paul realised he was losing ground and would be unlikely to have another such opportunity. So he made a concluding statement calculated to bring the proceedings to an end, and they dispersed.

It was a quotation from one of their own prophets, relating to the ministry to which he was called (recorded in Isaiah chapter six). When this is read in church services it is invariably concluded with, *"Here am I, send me"* (verse 8). Few realise or remember what an awesome task he was sent to fulfil. It was to preach for many years with terribly discouraging results. The people would hear, but not understand, see but not perceive. The more he spoke, the harder they would become and the less open to taking his message to heart. His ministry would actually make the situation worse rather than better! No wonder the prophet asked how long he would have to go on doing this, with such a negative effect, and the answer must have discouraged him: until the nation was destroyed, its cities ruined, its fields ravaged, its people scattered — until the national 'tree' was only a stump.

The implications of this mandate are shocking. Not only does God *know* this will be the appalling result, he is actually using this messenger to *make* it happen. He does not want his chosen people to 'turn and be healed'! His word has become an instrument of punishment rather than pardon, of justice rather than mercy, of rejection rather than acceptance. His people have backslidden beyond the point of no return. In passing, we may add a comment that such a divine action runs quite contrary to the contemporary sentimental notion of God's 'unconditional love' and would probably be dismissed as an 'Old Testament' view.

Yet Jesus quoted this very text from Isaiah as the rationale for his use of parables (Mark 4:11–12). The naïve explanation is that they were like sermon illustrations, intended to throw light on a subject and make the truth easier to understand and accept. On the contrary, Jesus himself said he was using them to *hide* the truth from those who did not want to hear it, to further *harden* their hard hearts and to prevent them repenting and being forgiven! He saw them in terms of judicial judgement comparable to Isaiah's prophecies. Only to those committed to following him did he explain the meaning, apparently lost to the general public, even taken from them (Mark 4:25).

Now Paul is quoting the same text. The majority of his hearers have become harder than they were before, even further from the truth. The tragic consequence is that they have lost the offer of 'salvation' Paul hoped to bring to them, and may never get another. Jesus is the door and they have slammed it shut. By contrast his preaching to the Gentiles has not had this negative effect. Isaiah's words only applied to Israel, as he, Jesus and Paul experienced.

So Paul bluntly announced that he would concentrate his time and effort on reaching and preaching to non-Jews, Gentiles, knowing that they would listen, perceive, understand, turn and be healed.

Apart from a final note recording Paul's continued preaching for the two years of his house arrest, this final incident with the Jews brings the book of Acts to a close.

******

It is time to summarise the findings of our study of Israel in Acts.

That 'replacement' theories find support in its pages is hardly surprising. First impressions are that it describes the transition of God's redemptive purposes from Israel to the church. It begins in the Jewish capital of Jerusalem and ends in the Gentile capital of Rome. The first half focusses on Peter, the apostle to the Jews; the second on Paul, the apostle to the Gentiles. Jesus diverts the attention of the apostles from a kingdom for Israel to a world mission. Peter castigates the Israelites for murdering their Messiah. Stephen appears to write them off as hopelessly stubborn and disobedient. James welcomes Gentiles into the church without insisting on the adoption of Judaism. Paul deliberately switches from Jews to Gentiles three times (the final occasion is thought to be the climax as well as the closure of Luke's account, a resumé of its message). Fittingly, as we have noted, its author, Luke, is the only Gentile author in our Bible.

It is an impressive case, leading to the conclusion that God has indeed transferred his agency on earth from one people to another, from one based on flesh to another based on faith. The latter may include a minority of Jews, but their membership will have nothing to do with physical heredity. The church is now the Israel of God.

However, a closer and more careful examination has

revealed a clear strand of hope for the future of Israel as a nation. We have shown that Jesus tacitly agreed that the kingdom would be restored to Israel. Peter likewise looked forward to a total restoration, which would include the fulfilment of every promise God had made to Israel, however long ago. James freely quoted the prediction of Amos that David's empire would be rebuilt. But there were indications that these events would be associated with Jesus' second coming rather than his first. They belong to the ultimate rather than the immediate future. They are no less certain for that.

A final comment on Paul. Did he, like Stephen, dismiss the Jewish people, believing that they had forfeited any possibility of being used by God, because of their rejection of his 'Holy and Righteous One'? Had they ceased to be his chosen people, now to be thought of and treated like any other nation?

If all the information we had about Paul was in Acts, we might speculate a positive answer to such questions. But it would be a grave mistake. Both his own reflections and unique revelations from God had led him to an exactly opposite conviction, as we shall see in the next chapter.

3

ISRAEL IN ROMANS

The division of the Bible into chapters and verses has caused many problems. It has spoilt the way we read Romans 9 – 11, suggesting that this section is separate from the rest of the letter — a kind of parenthesis or digression, when Paul talks about Israel. But it is nothing of the kind. There is a flow through the letter, and if you cut out the chapter divisions you can see this very clearly. For example, at the end of chapter eight (as we call it) it says that nothing can separate us from the love of God. But just a minute: were not the Jews separated from the love of God? No, says Paul. You see, if God could break a covenant with the Jews he could break a covenant with Christians. If he could get rid of them, he could get rid of us. So Paul immediately goes on to make it clear that God has not rejected the Jews. God does not do that. Do you see the connection?

Even more clearly, at the end of chapter eleven, Paul talks about God's mercy, his mercy already shown to

Gentiles; his mercy that is yet to be shown to Jewish people — because God wants to show his mercy to all mankind. Then, immediately, chapter twelve begins, *I beseech you, therefore, by the mercies of God, present your bodies as a living sacrifice.* Do you see that those chapter divisions have cut right into the flow of Paul's argument, the revelation God has given him?

Certainly chapters 9–11 are different from the others. The word 'Israel' starts being used with chapter nine, and it is used throughout these three 'chapters' (as we call them). So Paul is dealing with a specific subject. Furthermore, he starts quoting the Old Testament very freely with chapter nine. Indeed, there are thirty-seven different quotations from the Jewish scriptures in these three chapters. And many Christians have quite wrongly assumed: 'Ah, those chapters are for Jews, quoting their scriptures.' Actually, read all three chapters carefully and you see that they are not written to Jews; they are all written to Gentile believers. They are for us! Yet this little section in the middle of the letter is treated by scholars and preachers as though it is a unit in itself and can simply be left out of our thinking about Romans, and I am afraid that it frequently is.

Why did Paul include so much about Israel and the Israelites in his letter to the Romans? Why, particularly, in that letter? He could have done it in Ephesians. After all, Romans is already the longest letter, even without these three chapters. In fact, it is the longest letter ever written in the ancient world. We have no other letter that comes anywhere near as long. So why did he add to the length with this passage about Israel, which seems, on a superficial reading, to be a digression from his main teaching? Could it actually be the climax of the letter he is writing, its point and purpose? Could it be the most important part of the letter, that explains everything that is before it (1–8) and everything that follows it (12–16)? That is what I want to show you. It is the mountain peak of the letter. Everything before it builds up to this, and everything that follows works down and out from it.

Now the question people never seem to ask is: why did Paul write this very long letter? In my book *Unlocking the Bible*, I have tried to show that the context of every text in your Bible is the book in which it appears, not the chapter. And before you can understand anything in that book you need to know why that book was written. There are sixty-six books in your Bible and each one was written for a different purpose. Once you have found out why it was written you will understand everything in that book. Take the four Gospels: two of them were written for unbelievers (Mark and Luke); a third was written for young believers (Matthew), and the fourth was written for old believers (John). How you interpret the things in the Gospel depends on whether you are reading a Gospel written for unbelievers or young believers or old believers. Consider one example: the parable of the lost sheep. In Luke, which was written for unbelievers, the lost sheep is a lost sinner. But in Matthew, which was written for young believers, the lost sheep is a backsliding saint. Same story, different meaning in two different Gospels which were written for two different reasons.

It is comparatively easy with most of Paul's letters to determine why each one was written. You just need to read between the lines of his letter to find out why he wrote. Some crisis or situation had developed which needed a letter to cope with it. Correspondence corresponds to what is happening at the other end. It is like listening to a conversation that someone is having on a mobile phone and you cannot hear what the other person is saying. So your mind is constructing a situation at the other end of the phone. Have you done this? You are listening to someone: 'Well, congratulations! So it's arrived. How much does it weigh? What colour is it? And is it petrol or diesel?' You see what I mean? You were constructing a situation at the other end of the phone, and you were wrong! That is what we have to do with Paul's letters. We have to read them and ask what was going on at the other end, and in most of the letters it is very obvious. With Romans it is not so clear, and the result is that the scholars have been arguing about Romans for centuries and suggested at least twenty different theories as to why Paul wrote such a terribly long letter to the church in Rome.

We have to answer that question now if we are going to understand Romans 9–11. Something necessitated this letter, and there are two schools of thought. On the one hand, many people think that it was Paul who had a need to write this long letter to Rome, and there are five or six different ideas about why he needed to do so. One is that he had a preacher's ambition to preach in the great metropolis at the heart of the empire, and that he had begun to wonder if he would ever get there. In this way he was sending his sermon on ahead, so that at least they would get that from him even if he never got there in person. Another theory is that he was looking back on a lifetime's missionary work; he was wondering about his future, how much longer he had, and wanted to deposit a theology of the gospel in the main church in Rome where it could be referred to by all parts of the empire. Do you think Paul did that? Another theory is that Paul had now finished his mission in the eastern Mediterranean basin and was now planning to go west, beyond Rome. He says in the letter that he is planning to go on to Spain and that he needed a new base for his missionary work. Antioch, to which he reported back, was right in the eastern end and too far back. So he was hoping — so the theory goes — that Rome would become his new missionary base and support him to go further west to Spain. So he is presenting his credentials. They do not know him;

he has never been there. So he is saying: this is what I believe; are you willing to support my mission to the west? Is that right? Certainly, he wanted to go to Rome. He said that he had planned to go many times to them but had been thwarted by Satan so often. Was he then sending his gospel ahead for their approval or for their edification? I think all these theories that see the need at Paul's end are wrong. Paul never wrote for selfish reasons. He never wrote to promote himself. He said: I do not need letters of recommendation. My converts are my recommendation.

Therefore we must look at the other end of the correspondence and ask whether there was something happening in Rome that needed this very extensive letter from Paul at this stage. As soon as we begin to ask that, the situation begins to clear up enormously. Paul is not presenting his gospel in Romans. I want to say that because most Protestants think that is why he wrote it and therefore they think that what Paul says in Romans is the gospel which they ought to preach, and then they preach it. Actually Romans is not the gospel Paul preached, it is only part of it. There are many things that Paul preached as a fundamental part of the gospel which are not in Romans. For example, take the first big omission. There is next to nothing in the whole of Romans about repentance, yet Paul preached that more than anything else wherever he went. You probably know the verse where Paul writes, *I was not disobedient to the heavenly vision*. What was the heavenly vision he was not disobedient to? Most Christians have never noticed what he added. He continues: *so I preached repentance to the Gentiles that they should turn to God and prove their repentance by their deeds*. That is a crucial text on repentance. Repentance is not saying the sinner's prayer, it is proving you have turned from your sin and turned to God by your deeds — something you show, something you do. When he was on Mars hill he said: *God has overlooked your previous ignorance but now he commands everybody everywhere to repent*. There is nothing in Romans about heaven or hell; there is nothing about Jesus' return; there is nothing about the kingdom or the church; there is just nothing of what he normally preached. Yet people say Romans is Paul's gospel. It is no such thing. It is part of his gospel, but why does he miss out so much? Why does he only include parts? He is writing to people who are already converted. He is writing to believers who do not need the whole gospel, they have already had it, they have already responded to it. It is not a missionary tract. And if you build the whole gospel you preach on Paul's letter to the Romans you will miss out many important parts of his gospel.

So what was happening in the church at Rome? Let us ask *when* this letter was written. It was written in the early to mid 60s AD — thirty years after Jesus died, rose and ascended to heaven and sent his Spirit. Three decades have elapsed since all that happened on which the gospel is based. What has been happening in those thirty years? The answer is quite startling: **The church which Jesus is building has become more Gentile than Jewish.** And even though Paul's mission always went to the Jew first and then to the Gentile, as he said in Romans chapter one, he was having far more success with Gentiles. There were fewer and fewer Jews coming in, and more and more Gentiles. The church in Rome was a most peculiar example of this. It had gone through four phases of its life.

Phase number one was when the church in Rome began. It did not have an apostle to start it. Peter and Paul would come along much later, but there is no record of one of the twelve apostles going to Rome to start a church there. The only hint we have is that on the Day of Pentecost, when the Spirit was poured out, there were Jews and Jewish proselytes, or fringe members, of the synagogue from Rome. We can only presume that those among the three thousand converted, baptised, filled with the Spirit on the Day of Pentecost went back to Rome, their home, after the feast, and started a church, which means that in its first phase the Roman church was entirely Jewish.

Then the second phase came as they began to evangelise the city of Rome and Gentiles came in, and Gentiles accepted the Jewish Messiah as their Saviour and Lord. So in phase two the church in Rome was mixed, Jewish and Gentile.

Then phase three took a startling turn. The emperor Claudius, in the 50s AD, decided to banish all Jews from Rome. He did it for a very interesting reason: they were stirring up riots, they were causing a lot of civil unrest about a man called *Chrestus*, clearly Christ. Paul had found everywhere he went that there were some Jews who believed, but the majority did not and stirred up trouble with the Romans.

This was happening to a unique degree in Rome itself, and the Jews were getting very angry and disturbed because some of their number were joining this new sect and worshipping *Chrestus*. Because it caused so much trouble in the capital of the empire, Claudius, the emperor, said: Out with you! Whether you believe in *Chrestus* or not. And he banished all Jews from Rome. It is mentioned in Acts chapter eighteen. Among the Jews he threw out were a couple called Aquila and Priscilla, who went to Corinth and met Paul there.

Phase four came when Claudius died and Nero came to the throne. During his first years Nero was quite a good emperor. Claudius had left the economy in a bad state and Nero knew that Jews were good for the economy. He was not the last in the history of the world to invite Jews back for economic reasons. Cromwell did the same. So after Nero asked the Jews to come back, they came — most of them unbelievers, but some like Aquila and Priscilla returned. They are mentioned in Romans chapter sixteen as now back in Rome.

But when the Jewish believers got back and tried to reintegrate into the church they had been part of, the Gentiles did not want them. That is the situation behind Paul's letter to the Romans. They were not welcome. We can imagine the attitude: we don't want you Jews back in our fellowship; we are now a Gentile fellowship, and God is using us and blessing us; we don't need you. And there is no doubt that Aquila and Priscilla and one or two other of Paul's Jewish friends who had come back to Rome reported the situation to him and would have said to Paul: The situation is desperate; we need your help; we need you to come and bang our heads together! But Paul was planning to go to Jerusalem and he could not come. So what could he do? He could write a letter.

You did not write letters in the ancient world just to say, 'Having a lovely time, wish you were here!' because there was no mail. You could not just stick a stamp on a letter and push it in a mail box and expect it to get to the other end of the Roman empire next day or the following day. You had to find someone to take the letter there. It was a long and expensive business sending a letter. So Paul sat down to write a letter to deal with this potentially dangerous situation.

It was dangerous from many points of view. Here is

an insight you will not hear from other preachers. I have never found it in commentaries or books but it seems so obvious. While the Jewish believers had been away from the church in Rome for twelve years the preachers jumped to a conclusion that was terribly wrong: that God is finished with the Jews. 'This banishment from the capital of the empire is proof that he has rejected his ancient people and that he has chosen us Gentiles to replace the Jews. And we must be a good deal better than they are because God has kept us here and he is making us the new Israel.' Does this attitude sound familiar to you? It started in the church in Rome in the 50s AD. The whole letter of Romans is written against replacement theology, against the church as the new Israel. I am going to show you that the whole of the letter is written to deal with that crisis. Paul was so disturbed. First because it would mean a division in the church of Rome. It would mean the beginning of two separate denominations — a Jewish church and a Gentile church. And since all roads led to Rome, all roads led from Rome, and this division would spread throughout the empire. Paul had staked his ministry and mission on there being one new man in Christ Jesus, Jew and Gentile integrated, not worshipping separately but together. That was his concern. It was a desperate situation and it required wisdom, and tact, because he was going to have to write to a church he had not founded and had never visited. He had done that already, writing to the Colossians (having never been to Colossae). There too he was dealing with a church that did not know him, did not look up to him; he was not their father. So here in Rome he must go very carefully about rebuking them, because the Gentiles had become arrogant. He will deal with that in chapter eleven when he gets to it: three times he will rebuke them for their arrogance.

There is a downside to pride: if you put yourself up you will put others down, and the downside of arrogance is always contempt. And in the church at Rome they had developed a contempt for the Jewish people. It was the first seed of anti-Semitism in the church of Christ which would blight church history for the next two thousand years. I do not know if Paul realised where it would all lead, but he recognised what a dangerous situation it was — that the Gentile believers in Rome were thinking: God kicked the Jews out because we're better, because now we're his chosen people, and they are not. Clearly this had been preached and was widely believed during those twelve years when there were no Jews in the fellowship. Aquila and Priscilla and the others had come back into this atmosphere. It is no wonder they sent a message: Paul please come quickly! Paul made it clear that he could not do so. He was going to Jerusalem; it might be months, even a couple of years, before he could be present. If he waited until he had gone personally it would have been far too late and the damage would have been done. So he sat down and wrote this longest letter that had ever been written to try to nip that dangerous situation in the bud before it infected the whole church, before the church lost its Jewish roots and before the church became anti-Semitic and thought that God had changed one chosen people for another. How relevant that is.

So that was the situation that Paul was dealing with. It was the beginning of replacement theology, of anti-Semitism in the church, of Gentile arrogance towards the Jews, even among Christians. A desperate situation.

How would he get to it? Well, he does deal with the problem very directly in chapter eleven, as we shall see, where he rebukes Gentile arrogance toward the Jews three times in just one chapter. Has God rejected the Jews? Never! Have they fallen beyond recovery? Never! That word rendered 'never' is the strongest Greek negative you can imagine. He reveals then Christ's present and future plans for Israel. Because, he said, their arrogance was due to ignorance: you don't know about Israel's future and I'm going to tell you, because that will change your attitude. But this chapter is chapter eleven, which is a long way into the epistle. It is surely the climax of the first part of his epistle because he ends it with a doxology — praise to God — and he always does that when he has finished his strong teaching (as in Ephesians chapter three, for example). So it is an integral part of the teaching. It is not a parenthesis. He has been building up to this but he takes an awfully long time to build up to it. Why? I have told you the answer already. He is writing to people who do not acknowledge his authority, who have never known him as an apostle. Indeed, most of them have never seen him, they have only heard things about him. And they have probably heard things about him, as Paul himself realised, that were not very complimentary. So he must deal with them very carefully. And the first thing he must try to do is to keep them together. Before he deals with this thing that has come in and is about to wreck the future, he deals with the simple issue of their unity in the gospel. They are one in Christ Jesus, they cannot deny that. They are on exactly the same footing, Jew and Gentile. And he rebukes Jewish arrogance in chapter two and then Gentile arrogance later. But he is dealing with pride, which is the thing that can immediately break up Christian fellowship. So he spends the first eight chapters reminding them of their unity in the gospel, and he selects those aspects of the gospel which make them one. They are on exactly the same basis before God.

Let us just run through chapters 1–8 to show that what he is after is not, 'This is my gospel', but, 'This is the gospel that unites you and makes you one.' First of all he says in chapters 1–3: you are both sinners. Gentiles are sinners; Jews are sinners. You are all one because all have sinned and fallen short of the glory of God. He does acknowledge that the way they show their sinfulness is different. The Gentiles are more blatant, more crude, more decadent. He paints a picture of social breakdown and moral decay in chapter one that seems strangely modern, like a tabloid newspaper. He is saying: that is how you Gentiles sin before God. And, you Jews: the Gentiles did not have the commandments but they had a conscience, and their conscience they went against; but you had the commandments and you have gone against those. You have done it in a secret way. They do it openly; you do it inside and you hide it from other people. In conclusion: all have sinned. You Gentiles have sinned (chapter one); you Jews have sinned (chapter two); so (chapter three), all of you sinned. It is terribly important that we constantly remember that we have *all* been sinners, in different ways, but we are all starting there. That puts us humbly on an equal plane. You may have religion or you may not; that does not alter the fact you start before God as a sinner. The ground is level before God.

Then he moves on to God's solution to that problem. He said, the solution is the same for you both: justification by faith in the atoning death of his Son. Then he says, to push it home: for God is the God of the

Jew and of the Gentile; therefore you come to God the same way. Jews may have had historical advantages of revelation, the covenants, but they must come to God the same way Gentiles came. Gentile and Jew cannot be reconciled to God except through faith in Jesus' death and resurrection. So you are all the same; you were the same in sin, you are the same in salvation. Therefore in chapter four he teaches: you are all sons of Abraham, because the true sons of Abraham are not those who share his flesh but those who share his faith as well. And by faith there are not two groups, Jew and Gentile, there are not two kinds of sons of Abraham; all who share Abraham's faith are his sons. You see what he is saying all the way through? You are both sinners, you are both saved by grace through faith and you are both sons of Abraham — why are you dividing?

Then he points out: you both have the problem of reverting to your former life after you have become Christians. This is the danger of every Christian: that we slip back into our old ways. But once again he says that it is different for Gentile and Jewish believers because their past was different, and therefore slipping back into their past they do it in different ways. The Gentile believer is tempted to slip back into licence, into blatant sin; even justifying it, saying, 'Well, that will give God more to forgive.' Shall we sin that grace may abound? Never! That is the Gentile temptation, to slip back into licence, but it is not the Jewish temptation. They are tempted to slip back into legalism. So we find Paul dealing with Gentile backsliding in chapter six and telling them they must die to sin. But then in chapter seven he goes on to the Jewish converts and says they must die to the law. He lets them know: the law will kill you. And he gives a personal testimony as a Jew in chapter seven. This is what the law did to me. It was a good law, but it showed me that I was a greedy person. Is it not interesting that the one commandment Paul could not keep was the tenth? It is the hardest one of all. You shall not be greedy (covet). You cannot be content and covetous at the same time. If you covet, you are not content; if you are content, you do not covet — it is as simple as that. Godliness with contentment is great gain. But we live in a covetous society and it is a temptation to all of us. Paul says: it was a good law but it left me in guilt. So, Gentiles, don't go back into your old life of licence — die to sin. Jews, don't go back to your old life of law, legalism — die to law. As a woman is set free from the law of marriage as soon as her husband dies, you are set free by the death of Christ. So in chapter eight he says that what Jewish and Gentile believers both need is to live in the freedom of the Spirit. If you live in the flesh you die, but if you live in the Spirit, the law of the Spirit of life in Christ Jesus will set you free from the law of sin and death. And we have that magnificent chapter eight.

Do you see what Paul has been doing in these chapters? He is not preaching the gospel. There is no point in preaching to the converted. He is reminding them that Jew and Gentile are on exactly the same basis in relationship to God. They were both sinners. They both had to be justified by faith, and they both need to learn to live in the Spirit, the life that is freedom, and not slip back into the licence of Gentile life or the legalism of Jewish life. He is pleading for maintaining the unity of the gospel. The gospel has made them one. How dare they think of dividing!

The Jewish believers in Israel are one with us. They are saved from the same sin, by the same grace, to the same holiness, for the same eternity, all in the same Saviour. It is therefore an offence to the gospel when Jewish and Gentile believers worship separately. What a message! In other words, if you separate you are forgetting the gospel that made you one, and you will advertise a wrong gospel.

Jerusalem has suffered for centuries from Christian division. The Church of the Holy Sepulchre had at least five different Christian denominations in it, none of them would trust each other, so they had a doorkeeper of a different faith to look after the key. That is the kind of scandal the Jews have seen in Christian division. It is a denial of the gospel. Hear my heart in this. I am getting it from Paul. Hear his heart in this letter. He can see untold damage coming to the church if Jewish and Gentile believers cannot get on with each other.

Paul is nothing if he is not practical and he realises that you may be one in theory, but in practice that is a different matter. 'To dwell above with saints I love — that will be glory; to dwell below with saints I know, that's another story!' That is where Paul is so keen to work out our salvation in practice. Chapters 12–16 are precisely occupied with that. Many of Paul's letters start with doctrine and end with practical ethics. Ephesians is a classic case. Paul always comes down to earth and says now work it out. So, in Romans 12–16, Paul begins to show that he appreciates there are cultural differences when you have a mixed Jewish and Gentile fellowship.

There are going to be practical difficulties. He knew that, apart from anything else, they were living under the shadow of the emperor in Rome and there was going to be great pressure on them from the powers that be. So he spends chapter thirteen telling them that they must pray for the Roman authorities, pay their taxes and live as good citizens. But then he gets down to the problems and the pressures within the fellowship. And it is interesting that he does not then tell them the normal things about how husbands and wives should behave and how parents and children should behave, and how masters and slaves should behave. All that is in letters like those to the Ephesians and the Colossians but none of it here. Here he concentrates exclusively on those issues that would arise when Jews and Gentiles tried to live together as one body in Christ. So he mentions special days. And that is bound to come up. The Sabbath is bound to come up. He says some want to keep one day a week special. And he says others say, 'Oh, but every day is the Lord's day. I don't keep special days.' They are both free to do that. Sunday observance is not part of Christianity. We do not have a Sabbath law over us. But if one Christian wants to keep a day special, then fine; if others do not, fine. There is no law on Christians to have special days. And Christianity is free of festivals and special calendar feasts. The only reason why Christians celebrate Tabernacles is not because Jesus told them to, it is an act of friendship towards Jews; it is not a commandment. In fact, the church follows a Christian calendar but it should not. There is no command in scripture. There is nothing in the New Testament telling us to celebrate Christmas, but we do it. It is not part of being a Christian. For the Christian every day is the Lord's day — not one in seven, but seven out of seven.

Christians are not under the law of tithing either. If they do it, it is their free choice; it is the Mosaic law. There is no Christian commandment to tithe — though it is amazing how many churches manage their finances by teaching it. We are free of the law; we are under the law of Christ, under the guidance of the Spirit, and that is freedom. But when Jews and Gentiles get together the Jews are used to having Sabbath and used to having festivals and used to having special days. Paul says: you have got to learn to live together and allow each other the freedom to do this.

He also goes on to food and diet, and that is going to be a big issue when you have Gentile and Jewish believers together. In fact the Roman Catholic cardinal and the chief rabbi in London were at the Lord Mayor's Banquet together, and the cardinal said to the rabbi, 'I suppose I can't tempt you to a ham sandwich?' And the rabbi said, 'I'll have one at your wedding!' Which was a real rabbinic answer! Listen: Christians are going to have differences of conscience because conscience is culturally conditioned, and we have all got a conscience that was conditioned by the way we were brought up and what we were told by our parents was right and wrong. For years I would not ride a bicycle on Sunday because my parents told me it was a sin. I find now that in the Spirit I am free to ride a bicycle on Sunday. But I meet people who do not do some things on Sunday, and I have to live with them.

So, in Romans 12–15, Paul is working out these very practical matters. Having told them you are one in the gospel, you are one in sin, you are one in being justified by faith, you are all sons of Abraham, you are all tempted to revert to your own life, but you need to be one in the Holy Spirit's freedom, he teaches: but

I realise that when you sit down to a meal together, one of you wants kosher food and one doesn't. When you get to Friday, one observes the Sabbath and one doesn't. He said: love is the important thing. What he is saying in chapters 1–4 is: you are one faith. In chapters 5–8 he says: you are one in hope. In chapters 12–15, he says: you have got to be one in love, practical love, adjusting to each other, recognising people who have still got scruples in their conscience, adjusting your behaviour to theirs. That means the broad-minded adjusting to the narrow-minded, out of love. What a letter! And there in this whole letter which is working so hard, page after page, to keep them one, he suddenly says: now listen, I have got to talk to you about Israel. I have got to talk to you about the Jewish people, because God has not finished with them. Their rejection by Claudius was not a rejection by God. You have reached a very wrong conclusion.

I have to say that in my own country the majority of the church are living in that wrong conclusion. They think they have replaced God's chosen people, Israel. They dare to call themselves the new Israel, which the New Testament never does.

I have set out the context. Do you see how important context is? You now know why Paul wrote this whole letter. Therefore you will now understand this special section which is the climax — he has been building up to it — and chapter eleven is the real reason for the entire letter. But we can understand why he did not rush in. To charge into a church he had never been to and who did not know him, and say, 'You're wrong!' is the quickest way to lose friends and not influence people! When he wrote to the Galatians he knew them; he had fathered them; they were his spiritual children, and he goes straight in and says, 'If anybody brings another gospel to you, may he be cursed.' He does not hesitate; it is the only letter in which he does not thank God for them at the beginning, the only letter he never commends them for anything, because they are his children and he goes straight in and says: it is wrong. But you cannot do that with a church you have never been to. I have learned the hard way, you don't do that! You have got to establish a relationship, you have got to establish rapport before you can come right in with a hammer like that. Paul has done that, but we can see how skilfully he has laid the foundation; he really has worked very carefully to come to this particular section.

The whole letter is addressed to the Gentile believers in Rome. There are now Jewish believers back in the fellowship but it is not addressed to them. He sends them greetings in chapter sixteen — a lot of them, more than any other letter — to establish links with the fellowship. He says that he already knows a lot of them and asks for his greetings to be sent to Priscilla and Aquila and to all the others, a long list of about twenty-two names. But it is primarily addressed to Gentile believers. We have a letter in the New Testament entirely addressed to Jewish believers — the letter to the Hebrews, and it is written to Rome. Here in Romans there are references to the Jews but his main thrust is 'you' Gentiles and your arrogance toward the Jewish people.

Now Paul is going to deal with it directly. And the key to these three chapters is in the personal pronouns that he uses. First of all he uses the second person pronoun, 'you'. We know who 'you' is. He says, 'You Gentile believers'. So it is a very direct address. He has not used the word 'you' much until now, but now he is going to use it a lot.

Then he uses the third person pronoun 'they' to refer to the Jewish people — not just the Jewish believers but the Jewish unbelievers too. Whenever he says 'they' he is referring to Jewish people. Also in this section he uses the personal pronoun 'I' more than ever. He is getting very personal now, and each so-called 'chapter' (9, 10 and 11) begins with an outpouring of his personal feelings, 'I'. That is probably why the bishop who was responsible for chapter division divided the chapters and began each — 9:1; 10:1 and 11:1 — with Paul's heart, his emotions and outpouring. The second division is quite wrong as we shall see, and is misleading. He thought it would be a good idea to begin each chapter with this very personal and emotional outburst from Paul. So — you, they, I — these three pronouns govern the whole of these three chapters.

It is true that there are three major things that Paul is saying which roughly correspond to chapters nine, ten and eleven, but *only* roughly as we will see. But I want to give three headings: *In the past, Israel has been selected*. That is most of chapter nine. Then in chapter ten, where he moves on to another statement about God's ancient people, *In the present, Israel is being stubborn*. Thirdly, *In the future, all Israel will be saved*. That is most of chapter eleven. It is a historical review of his own people — of their past, of their present and of their future. This is his prime argument to deal with the Gentile believers' arrogance. In a sense he almost takes their side in chapters nine and ten. And had he stopped with chapter ten I am quite sure the Gentiles would have concluded that they were right, that God had rejected his people and that they were now the new Israel, God having replaced the Jews with them. But he did not stop at chapter ten, and thank God he did not. He told the whole truth. He admitted that in the present Israel was being very stubborn, even though in the past they were selected. He is going to say in chapter nine that not all Jews are God's Israel. I find different groups of Christians majoring on one of these three chapters and ignoring the other two, thereby getting into unbalanced thinking about Israel.

For example, Calvinist theology makes a huge amount of chapter nine. I have to confess I am not a Calvinist, and I have got news for you: Calvin wasn't either! Calvinism today comes from his successor, Theodore Beza, but that is a whole different story. But in chapter nine we have a remarkable picture of God's sovereignty — that he has mercy on whom he chooses, that he hardens whom he chooses, as if it is so arbitrary that it is a matter of luck whether you get saved or not! And ultra Calvinism has built so much on chapter nine, as much as to say, and they do say, that whether a man or a woman is saved or not depends on God's choice and nothing else, that nothing in the person influences God. God picks a name out of a hat and says, 'I'll save him', picks another name out of a hat and says, 'I'll harden him and send him to hell.' That is such a travesty that I believe it is libellous against God. It means that God does not want to save everybody, and that is not the God I have got to know. The God I know wills that all men should be saved; he wants everybody in his family. To say that he is choosing some and damning others is I believe wicked. But it is built on Romans chapter nine where it seems to say that God chooses this one and not that one regardless of anything in them at all, which makes salvation a matter of pure luck, from a human point of view. They have ignored Romans chapter ten which says that we are responsible for being lost. And Romans chapter eleven says God wants to have mercy on all mankind. You see the danger of taking chapter nine and ignoring chapter ten and ignoring chapter eleven? That is what ultra Calvinism has done and it has swept through the Christian church like a dose of salts.

Then there are 'replacement' theologians who make an awful lot of chapter ten and ignore chapters nine and eleven. They point to Paul's admission that the Jews were stubborn, that it is their own responsibility that they had refused the gospel and turned their backs on it and rejected their own Messiah. So the replacement voice says: that's it, they had their chance and they missed it and now God has given us the chance and we have taken it, so we have replaced them. They ignore chapter nine and God's sovereign choosing of Israel, which he does not go back on, and they ignore chapter eleven, but they build their theology on chapter ten.

Then Zionists build on chapter eleven and ignore chapters nine and ten! How often have I sat in their Christian Zionist meetings and heard chapter eleven quoted. I have not once heard chapter ten quoted, nor chapter nine. Because chapter nine says *all Israel is not Israel*. And it is assumed too easily in Zionist circles that all the Jews are God's 'Israel'. Chapter nine says they are not and we need to face that. Furthermore, Zionists are prone to ignore chapter ten where Paul says that his heart and longing is to save some Jews. But there are Zionists who are almost committed not to evangelise Jews. Yet there are Jews dying today and going into a Christ-less eternity and they are lost. Listen: we can be supporters of Israel but we are still to long and work for the salvation of every Jew. They are a lost people, they have missed it and they need Christ. Yet I was told on one occasion at an arranged meeting, 'Don't talk about Christ, there are Israelis in the audience.' Whenever I speak to Jews I always talk about Jesus, and they have never objected, because they know I am doing it out of love. Maybe I am exaggerating but I am trying to show you that taking chapter nine out of its context, or taking chapter ten out of its context, or taking chapter eleven out of its context leads us into difficult and dangerous waters. Take the whole of scripture, take the whole of Romans, take the whole of 9–11, and we will get a balanced view. So, while nine and ten are not very good news for a Christian Zionist, eleven is, but we have got to get the bad news before we get the good news; we have to work through it steadily.

IN THE PAST, ISRAEL WAS SELECTED

Chapter nine is divided into two parts — the same two parts as chapter eleven. It begins by looking at the Israel of God but then finishes by looking at the God of Israel. That is a good order. You can get so preoccupied looking at the Israel of God that you get out of focus and you need your eyes lifting again to the God of Israel.

But we start then in chapter nine with the Israel of God. I want to start with two English poets. One was called William Norman Ewer. He lived in the middle of the nineteenth century, and he wrote a couplet which has become world famous: 'How odd of God to choose the Jews.' I am sure you have heard that poem quoted. It was published 150 years ago and it has gone round the world. There was another English poet called Cecil Brown, and since Ewer's was such a short poem he decided to add a second verse: 'But not so odd as those who choose a Jewish God and spurn the Jews.' I love those two little poems and they summarise chapter nine of Romans. 'How odd of God to choose the Jews, but odder still for those who choose a Jewish God and spurn the Jews.' You cannot have one without the other. You cannot have God without Israel and you cannot have Israel without God. If you chose a Jewish God you have to deal with Israel because he is the God of Israel. The Israel of God and the God of Israel go together. That is the message of chapter nine. That is why the patriarchs come into it. And to claim their God and to ignore them, or have contempt for them, is a contradiction in terms. It is like talking of a square circle or frying snow — you can't do it! It is crazy to say, 'I believe in God but don't love the Jews' — you just cannot do it.

Let us look at the first half — the Israel of God in chapter nine. Paul approaches the whole thing indirectly. He is wanting to talk about their feelings about the Jews, so he begins by talking about his feelings about the Jewish people. Of course he is a Jew, but the way they have treated him you would expect him to be resentful and bitter, and to say he was finished with them. Time after time, Paul had been hounded out of synagogues, hounded out of cities by being reported to the Roman authorities. He had no greater enemy than his fellow Jews. He was a traitor in their eyes. He had turned away from their God to this new Jesus. You would have thought that Paul's natural, fleshly reaction would be, 'I thank God I'm free of them.' But no, he calls God to witness: *I speak the truth in Christ — I am not lying, my conscience confirms it in the Holy Spirit*. Paul knows the readers will doubt what he is going to say next. He is calling on Father, Son and Holy Spirit as guarantors of it. Paul is in agony daily. He is in anguish for his people, the Jews. This is opposite to the attitude he is going to deal with later, but he is going right in now; he is baring his heart. He says, *I could*

*wish that I myself were cursed and cut off from Christ
for the sake of my brothers . . . .*

Do you feel that about unsaved relatives? There
is a passion here. Jesus, *redeemed us from the curse
of the law by becoming a curse for us*, but of course
Paul could not do that; Jesus could, and he did. Jesus
went through hell for me, did you know that? Hell is a
very dark place — there is no light there — and Jesus
was in darkness for three hours on the cross. Hell is
a very thirsty place and Jesus cried out, 'I'm thirsty.'
And hell is a lonely place because God is not there.
And Jesus cried out: *"My God, my God, where have
you got to?"* Jesus went through hell so you could go
to heaven. And that same passion and willingness to
go to the utmost lengths to save others is what Paul is
bearing in his heart for Jews, his own people. What a
revelation! Far from being bitter and resentful at the
way his fellow countrymen have treated him all his life
since his conversion, he is in daily anguish for them
and he wants the Gentile believers in the church in
Rome to know this. Whether they believe it or not, he
just calls on Father, Son and Holy Spirit — tell them
I'm telling the truth! I don't lie; my conscience is clear.
The Holy Spirit confirms I am in anguish.

His anguish is due to the fact that they had such
privileges and such advantages over Gentiles. God
had invested so much in them. He says theirs are the
covenants, theirs are the patriarchs. They have got

everything they needed. The divine glory was given to them. They have the adopted sonship. They received the law. They had the temple worship. The Messiah, humanly speaking, was a Jew. They had everything, and they have got nothing. What anguish, that God should have given them so much, and that they should have turned it all down. We notice that when he says theirs was the Messiah, humanly speaking, he immediately adds: *who is God, praised for ever*. That was the difference, that was what the Jews could not and would not accept, that *Yeshua* was God. They knew he was human, but he claimed to be God. They crucified him because he said he was God. The reason why Jesus was put to death is very simple: what was seen as blasphemy, because he implied again and again: I am the God of Israel. A carpenter from Nazareth!

The Jews had everything, and finally God sent his own Son, who was a Jew and always will be. But he was also God who is praised for ever, and that was the bit they could not cope with, and because of that they lost the rest.

Paul has to deal with an immediate question. Does this mean that God made a mistake with the Jews? Does this mean that God wasted all that investment in their history? Does this mean that God has gone back on his word? Never. The thing we have to realise is that God did not need them all. In fact, in God's sight they are not all his chosen people; not all Israel's descendants are

Israel. That is a bit of a shock. We are so used to using 'Israel' inclusively as a name, either for the political nation, or less commonly for all the Jews scattered in the diaspora as well. But, for us, Jew equals Israel — not to God. And we are going to have to grapple with that statement if we are going to understand the Christian attitude to Israel correctly. *Not all Israel is Israel* means quite simply, not all human Israel is the divine Israel. We must ask: what is God saying? And what does this mean? I plead with you to read Romans 9–11 before continuing.

We now take a closer look at chapter nine. It appeared as though there had been a terrible mistake. It seemed as if God had failed. He should never have tried it with the Jews. They were just the wrong people to choose: they had failed God, and God would have been much better off starting with Gentiles. That was how the Gentile believers were thinking in the Roman church. Furthermore, it is not just that 'Israel' has failed God, but the God of Israel has failed them, because he has failed to keep them. He has lost them. So he has broken his covenant, broken his word, broken his promises. This was what the Gentile preachers in Rome were saying.

Paul tells them that they are wrong. He makes a statement to correct their thinking, which I have never heard quoted at any Christian Zionist meeting, because it cuts right across many of our assumptions: God has

not failed. It was not a mistake. It has not all ended
in disaster, because not all Israel's descendants are
'Israel'. Or, to put it in very simple language, not all
Jews are Israel. That turns your thinking upside down,
because people use the word 'Israel' so loosely today
that I want to challenge them when they say, 'I love
Israel'; 'We support Israel'; 'We want to serve Israel.'
I want to ask, 'Who do you mean? Are you thinking
of Israel in human terms, or in divine terms? Are you
using that name as people use it, or as God uses it?' Let
us look at some of the ways that Christians use the term
'Israel'. Many use it in a geographical sense. 'Have
you been to Israel?' What do they mean? They mean
to a place in the Middle East about the size of Wales,
called Israel. They are talking about a geographical
Israel. That is not God's 'Israel'. Then there are those
who use the term 'Israel' in a political way. They are
referring to a modern state, a political entity called
Israel, and when they say 'we support Israel' they are
meaning we support a political state called Israel. That
is not God's Israel. But many people confuse it. Then
there are those who get a little deeper into it and use
it in a racial sense, or a national sense would be next,
meaning Israelis, citizens of the State of Israel — 'we
love Israel' and 'we support Israel' meaning we support
Israelis. But that is not how God thinks. Then there are
those who have the definition of Israel in racial terms,
meaning all Jews, and not just Israelis in the State of

Israel, but the majority of Jews who live elsewhere. It is estimated that about 40% of Jews live in Israel; many are scattered throughout the world in the diaspora. When you say 'we love Israel, we support Israel, we are friends of Israel' do you mean all the Jews in the world, including those in your own country? That is still not God's idea.

Paul is saying here, quite simply, that human definitions of Israel are not God's Israel. Not all Israel's descendants are Israel.

Are you beginning to think, 'Let us wrestle with this'? Who did Paul mean by 'Israel' the first time he says, 'All Israel's descendants'? Of course, he means Jacob. But he means Jacob after God had broken him, and made him a prince and the father of twelve sons who became twelve tribes of Israel, and God changed his name from Jacob to Israel. But I am sure he is also including the Israel that the twelve tribes and the nation became, and he is referring not just to Jacob's descendants but the descendants of his descendants. Put them all together, and they are *not* all Israel. God looks at the Jews, and he says some of them are Israel and some are not. And it is very important for us to grasp this: when God uses the word 'Israel' he is not referring to the land, to the political state, to all Israelis, or all the Jews throughout the world. He is referring to *some* of them. He has chosen, out of Israel's descendants, those who are *his* Israel. And we must think of Israel in God's terms, and see Israel through his eyes, and not as the world sees Israel today.

From the beginning it has never been the case that all the descendants of any of God's chosen people belong to his Israel. So, immediately after this statement, Paul goes right back to the beginning, to Abraham. Now, Abraham had eight sons, and only one of them was Israel. He had Ishmael first, after an act of adultery, but it was common practice in those days to have sex with one of your maidservants if your wife could not produce a child, and Abraham fell into that habit, but it was an act of adultery, and Ishmael was the result. Ishmael was not part of God's children, but not because he was illegitimate — that was not the reason. And when Sarah died, Abraham married Keturah and he had six more sons, and none of them were in God's Israel. Only one of Abraham's sons was part of God's people, and the other seven were not. Now, if you think it was because Ishmael was illegitimate, the next generation will correct your thinking, because Isaac had twins. They were both legitimate. They were so close, they were not just half brothers, they were twins, and yet only one of them was God's Israel, and the other one was not.

Paul quotes the Old Testament, *"Jacob I have loved and Esau I have hated."* Before you draw wrong conclusions there, 'love' and 'hate' to God are not emotions but actions. It is a word that means choosing to relate to someone and choosing not to relate to someone else, which is why Jesus said that you are not worthy to be his disciple if you do not 'hate' your father and mother. That has been widely misunderstood, but it means that if your Lord wants one thing and your parents want another, you turn away from your parents and you do what the Lord wants. That is love and hate in biblical terms. We tend to think they are emotions, and you feel nice towards somebody and nasty towards somebody else. That is not what it is at all.

Of these twin brothers, God chose one and not the other to be in his people. And it was not because of the way they turned out later. Paul said that. It was not because Esau turned out to be bad and Jacob good, far from it. Jacob was as bad as Esau, if not worse. But God chose one and not the other. And, you notice, all the way down the line he is not choosing the one who would be the natural choice. It was always the elder brother who would take over the father's business and inherit from the father, not the younger. God chooses people who have no desert or merit before him. He loves to do that. He loves to take nobodies and make them somebodies. He loves to take those who have got nothing and give them something. That is God. And you see all the way down from the very beginning, all descendants are not God's. And, ever since, all Israel's descendants are not Israel. So please start thinking of Israel as God thinks. God's Israel are those he has chosen from among the Jews, who have responded to his choice in the right way.

God's original choice of Jews, or some of them, was not for *salvation* but for *service*. That is a very important point. God's election of Israel was not to eternal salvation but to temple service in this world. He needed agents, instruments, vessels to hold his revelation for the whole world and through whom he could bless everybody else. That was his original choice, and we ought to remember it whenever we see the word 'election', or 'predestination'. We are going to have to grapple with predestination and freewill, and you know what a subject that is for teasing your brain!

But God chose them. It was those who responded to his call and his choice in trust and obedience who became his Israel. Abraham responded in faith, so did Isaac, so did Jacob, even though God had to deal with him very seriously and he limped for the rest of his life. But the limping Jacob was more use to God than the strong young man who tried to bargain with God and said: I'll give you a tithe of all that I possess if you bring me back safely. God does not respond to people who try to strike bargains with him. 'Lord, if you will do that, I will do this.' I have known so many people do that. Soldiers during world wars used to say, 'God, if you get me out of this and back to my family I will go to church every Sunday.' They tell me they did that. That is Jacob. Thinking he can bargain with God, thinking he has got something that he can pay to God to twist God's arm to help him; and God waits until Jacob has nothing, and Jacob is weak. God has broken this man and now he says: you can be my Israel. Ever since, it is those descendants of Jacob, of Israel, who respond to God's call in trust and obedience, who are his Israel. That is not the last word on this point, as we will see in chapter eleven.

We have seen Paul's anguish about what I have called the tragic irony of Israel. We have seen her treasured inheritance which God had given. And we have seen now her true identity. It is much smaller than the way the world thinks of Israel. But I want to reassure you that does not mean that God has failed. The simple fact is that God does not need all of them to fulfil his purpose. God is not interested in numbers. Gideon had to find that out. God can do more with a few dedicated men who will do what he tells them than he can with the whole nation. All the way through, it is God's remnant within Israel through whom he has accomplished his purpose. He has done what he promised, not through the whole lot but through that remnant who responded to his call and choice, in trust and obedience.

It is still true today. There has never been a time in the last two thousand years when there has not been a remnant of Jews responding to God in trust and obedience, and *they* are his Israel. Notice that God decides who belongs. He makes the first move. There are two aspects of the call of God. There is God who calls, and there are people who respond by calling on him. Both are mentioned in Acts chapter two, where Peter talks about God calling — that he would give the Holy Spirit to everyone whom he calls — but he also adds the other side, *"And whoever calls on the name of the Lord shall be saved."* There are two calls needed for God's Israel. The call of God, his choice, and the call back, calling on the name of the Lord for salvation.

We have looked at the Israel of God, and found it is not quite the Israel we thought it was. Now we look at the God of Israel. And Paul begins to talk about God's free will, and God's rights to choose. But if there is one thing that is offensive to human thinking it is that God has free will, that God should make the choice of his people. We want to be self-willed, we want to choose ourselves. We want to be in charge. So Paul now engages in what is called a theodicy, which means a justification of God — justifying God's ways before people. And he says God has a perfect right to choose. He has more free will than we have, but that the essence of sin is to say to God: 'Not your will but mine be done.' 'I did it my way' is the national anthem of all sin. I was in Berlin with Cliff Richard (whom I baptised, incidentally). He was a member of our fellowship. In

Berlin he sang a wonderful song called *I Did It His Way*. And it went down well. It was a wonderful song, which he had written himself. He had adopted the tune, of course, but he had changed the words. I am afraid he only sang it once in his lifetime because he was then told that he did not have the copyright to the tune and could not sing his words to it unless he sang *I Did It My Way*, so the song has never been heard anywhere else, except on that one occasion. But I know Cliff well, and he does it the Lord's way. God has a free will. We want to feel that we are in charge of the universe. We make a choice, but it is his will, and it was when his Son said 'Not my will but yours be done' that our salvation became possible.

So Paul now anticipates a reaction to what he has been saying about God choosing Jacob and not Esau, and God choosing Isaac and not the other seven. He feels that people would begin to say it is not fair. Now, I had three children (two are still on earth, one is in heaven) and they learned to say something which we did not teach them. Long before anybody taught them, they said, 'It's not fair.' And I do not know where they learned this from, but some people go on saying that for the whole of their lives.

I meet people every day who are faced with more serious problems. 'Why did God take my child?' 'Why did God break up our marriage?' 'Why did he let it happen?' 'Why is he letting terrorists get on with it?'

'Why? Why? It is not fair. We do not deserve it.' It is there all over the world. And sure enough, when you talk about God choosing one and not another, it is thought unfair. And Paul has an argument now about the justice of God. He has to, to lay a foundation for what he is going to say later. He makes the point that anything we get from the Lord is undeserved. It is always his mercy. My wife introduced me to a bad habit when we married. She cannot get going without a cup of tea in the morning. It is her daily 'fix'. So, when we married, this is what began to happen. If I wake up and feel like a Christian I go down and make the tea. And if I wake up and do not feel like a Christian, I wait until she goes and makes the tea. It is a very good arrangement. I must admit, I do not often feel like a Christian first thing in the morning. But when I go down, I go outside and I pick up two bottles of milk. (We get our milk delivered to the door.) I clutch them, and come back in, and I always think of a text from Lamentations: *Your mercies are fresh every morning*. And I thank God for his mercies. I come in and I thank the Lord. I am healthy. I do not deserve to be, it is a mercy. It is not a right. I have got a job to do; I have work to do. That is not a right. It is a mercy. I have a roof over my head, we have a house of our own, and that is not a right, it is a mercy. His mercies are fresh every morning, because if God dealt with me as I deserve I would not be a teacher, and you would not be reading this. It is by his mercies that we are not consumed. Nobody deserves anything but justice from God and, frankly, that frightens me. I do not want justice from God. Mercy is entirely at the disposal of the one who shows it. If it is undeserved, nobody has a right to it, and if God chose to have mercy toward someone and not to someone else, that is not injustice.

The parable of the labourers in the vineyard is one of my favourite parables. The owner of the vineyard did justice for everybody. Everybody got a full day's wage. Everybody got justice, but the owner of the vineyard chose to give more to some who did not deserve it, and when those who had worked all day only got a day's wage, they said: it is not fair; that is not just. And he said it was his money he was giving away. Don't I have a right to do what I want with my money? If I choose to give some more than they deserve, that is not injustice. I am being more than fair, not less.

That is God, and we must stop arguing, saying it is not fair if God shows mercy to this person and not to that, since none of us deserves it, none of us has a right to it. It is God who chooses who receives his mercy.

This is in both the Old Testament and the New. Paul is quoting from Deuteronomy: *"I will have mercy on whom I will have mercy."* So God does not love the Jews because they are loveable. God loved them, he said, because he loved them. God does not love you because you are loveable. He loves you because he loves you. He has mercy on you because, *"I will have mercy on whom I will have mercy."* Get God's angle on all this. But it is instinctive in the fleshly mind to argue with God, and tell him he is not being fair and tell him he is not being just. Paul has to deal with all this here. It is not fair for you to choose some and not others.

Then Paul teaches: God is perfectly free to harden people, as well as show mercy. He is absolutely within his rights to be tender towards some and tough towards others. Now, this really upsets his hearers. Paul writes, *One of you will say to me: "Then why does God still blame us?"* (9:19, *NIV*.) He has been through these arguments with so many other people. He knows what they are thinking, and he anticipates the objection, because now somebody asks: if God decides whether to be tough or tender with me, how can he bring me to account? How can he charge me? I am not responsible, if God decides what I am to be. Again, it is a human argument: that God is not being fair in deciding whether to show mercy or hardness, and then saying now you must come and stand and be judged before me. The objector implies: you should not be judging me; you decided what I would become; I am not responsible, you are. Now, Paul deals with this objection, but not quickly. He deals first with the attitude behind that kind of question, and I have found that often, when people argue with my teaching, I am not so worried about the argument as the attitude behind the argument. You may answer one question, one objection, quite satisfactorily, and immediately another objection is raised, and one thinks: you do not want to believe, do you? You are going to raise objection after objection because you have already decided you are not going to believe what you are hearing.

So Paul deals with the attitude before he answers the objection: Who do you think you are? The clay does not talk to the potter like you talk to God. You are a creature and he is the Creator who made you. How dare you be so cheeky, so impudent as to try to teach God his business. Any complaint, such as 'Why does God do this?' if you are not careful, develops an attitude that I could do a better job than he does if I were God. Every argument against God boils down to the fact that I think I know better, and he is accountable to me, and answerable to my little brain for what he does. The attitude is wrong. But Paul does not leave us there. Unfortunately, as we have already noted, Calvinists tend to stop at that point and they develop a theory about God, a theology which I think is dreadful. They have developed the theory that, in matters of eternal salvation, we are entirely at the mercy of an inscrutable God, and that it is a lottery whether you get saved or not — if God pulls your number out, you will be saved, and you cannot do anything about it and you cannot ever slip from grace because he forces you to be converted, and he will force you to stay with it. That is strict Calvinism.

Grace is not an irresistible force. It is an undeserved favour. But when it is taught as an irresistible force, that God has a big hat with all our numbers in, and he pulls one out and says, 'I'll have mercy on him,' pulls another, 'I'll harden him,' that is totally arbitrary, and it means that we have no idea who God will choose to be saved or not. It means also that God does not want everyone to be saved, and that is a lie, because scripture says he does. It means that mercy is pure chance as to whether you get it or not. I do not believe it. So we must say more. Paul teaches that God has an absolute right to choose to show mercy to someone and to harden another since, as he said earlier in the letter, we are all sinners and none of us deserves anything from God — but that is not Paul's last word on God's choice, and it must not be for us. I am not a fatalist, which is the other side of 'luck' and 'chance'. I believe that God's mercy is shown in an understandable way, and his hardening is shown in an understandable way. It is not inscrutable.

So Paul goes on, having established that we must not have the attitude 'I am just and God is unjust, and I can argue the case.' Get rid of that attitude, and then we find something rather different: that God only hardens those who have already hardened themselves against him. What if, as Paul teaches, God shows great patience before he hardens anyone? Of course, Pharaoh comes immediately to mind. In fact, Paul has already said God hardened Pharaoh's heart, and that is true. But if you study the book of Exodus carefully you will find that Pharaoh's heart was hardened ten times over the ten plagues. And you will find that the first seven times Pharaoh hardened his own heart against God. It was only with the last three that God helped Pharaoh along the road he had himself chosen, because then God could use Pharaoh for another purpose: to demonstrate divine power. It is all there. God does not pick a name out of a hat and say: I'll harden him or her. Not at all. He only hardens those who have already set their hearts like stone against all appeal from him. That is what happened to Pharaoh, and God has the right to do this. In effect he is saying: if I cannot use you for one purpose, I will use you for another. But I am still God.

Now, Paul has used the analogy of the potter and the clay, but that comes from the book of Jeremiah, and if you read Jeremiah chapter eighteen you find that the prophet was told go to the potter's house and watch him. So he went to the potter's house which overlooked the Valley of Ben Hinnom. The potter took a lump of clay and he put it on the wheel, and he tried to mould it into a beautiful vase. But the clay would not run in his hands, and he could not make this delicate vase, so he took the lump of clay and formed it into a lump again, threw it on the wheel and made a crude, thick, common pot out of it. *Then the word of the LORD came to me* [Jeremiah]: *"O house of Israel, can I not do with you as this potter does?" declares the LORD. "Like clay in the hand of the potter, so are you in my hand, O house of Israel. If at any time I announce that a nation or kingdom is to be uprooted, torn down and destroyed, and if that nation I warned repents of its evil, then I will relent and not inflict on it the disaster I had planned"* (Jeremiah 18:5–8, *NIV*).

The Lord wanted to make Israel a beautiful vessel, full of his mercy, but they would not run in his hands. So he was going to make them a crude pot, full of his judgement. He would use them, one way or the other. If Israel repented and changed, he would make them back into a beautiful vase, but if they did not, they would become a crude pot to illustrate his justice, not his mercy. That was their choice. Jeremiah was told to go back the next day to the potter, and when he went back, there was the crude pot. It had been out in the sun for a day, and it was now hard. Impossible now to change its shape. And he was told to go to the edge of the Valley of Ben Hinnom and throw it down until it crashed to pieces, because now it was too late. The clay was no longer soft.

Jesus used the Valley of Ben Hinnom as a picture of hell. God wants to make every human being a beautiful vessel, full of his mercy, and men say, 'No, I do not want to be that.' God says: well, you harden your heart, I will help to harden it. And his sun will shine on that life until it becomes so brittle that there is no hope of it changing. That is God. And that is what he wanted with Israel. They would not run in his hands. I do not see any injustice in that, do you? God, as soon as a person responds to his mercy, will soften that heart, but if the heart says no, I do not want it, I will do my own will, then the hardness comes in and there comes a point where God says: if that is what you want I will help you to be hard, and I will use you to demonstrate my power. And he does.

So Paul did not stop there, and he now shows God's mercy is directed, and how he exercises his power. God will be very, very patient with those who are hardening their hearts, but if they are utterly set on that course he will then demonstrate his power and judgement through them, as he did with Pharaoh. Pharaoh could have been saved. Pharaoh could have changed his mind. Pharaoh could have said, after five, six, seven plagues, 'I will let you go', but he did not. Seven, of course, is the perfect complete number in scripture, and seven times Pharaoh said no. He changed his mind and would not let them go. So God would demonstrate his power by destroying Pharaoh's army when they chased after his people.

In the last part of chapter nine, we move from how God exercises his power to how God extends his people. Here we have the first big surprise: that even the prophets Hosea and Isaiah realised that God's mercy would reach few Jews and many Gentiles. It was known right back then. God, of course, knew what would happen, and he revealed to Hosea and to Isaiah that there would be many Gentiles in 'Israel' and few Jews in his 'Israel'. The prophets saw all along that that would be God's people, and that is what has happened. There are thousands of Jews in God's people today, but there are millions of Gentiles. The prophets spoke about it. You will never understand the New Testament until you know your Old Testament. They belong together as the Word of God. So it should be no surprise to us that there are so many Gentiles and so few Jews in God's people.

With verse 39, we come to a new subject. And that is why the chapter division is wrong. Unfortunately, as I told you, the chapter divisions are made by Paul's emotions and in 10:1 again he lays bare his heart, but the real division comes between v. 29 and v. 30. He is now going to answer the big question: *why* are there so few Jews and so many Gentiles? It was already true in Paul's day. By the late 60s AD, thirty years after the death and resurrection of Jesus, there were ten times more Gentiles than Jews in God's people. And today it is a far greater racial proportion: millions to thousands.

So why? Whose fault is it? Whose responsibility is

that? Is it, as you might imagine from chapter nine, that God chose only a few Jews and many Gentiles? No. That again would be totally arbitrary. That would be the lottery again, as if God said, 'I just want a few Jews and a lot of Gentiles.' No. So whose responsibility was it? The answer is, it was the responsibility of the Jews *and* Gentiles. It was the responsibility of the clay, not the potter. Now, this is why we must keep chapters nine, ten and eleven together. If you only have chapter nine, you come up with this Calvinist concept of God who just picks people out for salvation and leaves the rest, but you must link the divine sovereignty in chapter nine with the human responsibility in chapter ten. It is the other side of the coin. No-one goes to hell because God chooses it. God did not want a single human being in hell. He made hell. He had to, for the evil angels and the devil. He has prepared it for them. He does not want any human beings to finish up there. God does not choose some for heaven and some for hell. That is a slanderous libel on God, because the ultimate deciding factor as to who finishes in one place or the other is a human responsibility.

The fact that there are so few Jews in God's 'Israel' is the Jews' responsibility and not God's. Let us get that absolutely clear. Yes, he did choose for service one out of Abraham's children, one out of Isaac's children, and a few out of Israel's descendants, but they all had the opportunity to be part of it, and it was

139

their responsibility if they are not, just as it is Gentiles' responsibility whether they are included or not in God's people.

IN THE PRESENT, ISRAEL IS STUBBORN

We now move to the second section of chapters nine to eleven. In the past, Israel was selected; in the present, Israel is stubborn. And we have to speak the truth here: God is not responsible for this difference of proportion. He wanted every Jew to be part of his Israel, but many have refused. Not because he did not choose most of them, but because most of them did not choose him. Or rather, most of them did not choose his Messiah. There are two issues that we must look at now: righteousness and revelation. It is in relation to these two that we come to the answer to the question: why are so few Jews in God's 'Israel' today? People who represent God must reflect him. They must be 'like' him if people are to realise what God is like. That is why God said to the Jewish people, *"Be holy, for I am holy."* But that same thing is said to Christians. The standard of righteousness in Judaism is high and difficult. There are ten big commandments and 603 little ones, affecting all of life. Those laws of Moses are remarkable. If you get dry rot in your house you must burn the house down, out of love for your neighbour. Do you fancy doing that? I am breaking a law of Moses now, because Moses said that you must not wear clothes of mixed material, and my garment is partly wool and partly some man-made fibre. So I am breaking the law of Moses. It is a very difficult standard of righteousness. You may have noticed that in hotels in Israel the lifts have Sabbath buttons, because pressing an electric button, according to the Chief Rabbi, is work, and you must not do that on the Sabbath. It is not work to climb ten flights of stairs, but it is work to press an electric button. This is the ridiculous legalism that you get into when you try to live out Moses' law. There is not a Jew alive today who is keeping Moses' law. There are many trying hard to do so, but there is not one alive who is managing it.

The Christian standard of righteousness is higher still: not only that you must not murder people, but you must not wish them dead, or call them a fool; not just that you must not commit adultery, but you must not even think about it, you must not even imagine it. Jesus' standard of righteousness is so high as to seem impossible! Who can live the Sermon on the Mount? I cannot. I do not think I could ever keep all of the Jewish law, and Moses said you have to keep all these laws all your life. But take note: Judaism, like every other religion in the world, says you have got to do it yourself. This produces and encourages self-righteousness. And this kind of 'self-righteousness' is very unlikely to be managed on the inside, though you might manage it on the outside! Do-it-yourself righteousness defeats its own object, because the more righteous you manage to become, the more hypocritical and the more proud you may be.

Pharisees are not popular, and they are trying so hard to be righteous. Our gospel, according to Romans, is able to save people who *go on believing* because in it is revealed *the righteousness of God*. The difference between Christianity and all other religions is that all other religions say you must *try* to be righteous. Christianity says the opposite: stop trying, and get the righteousness of God. *Let him do it in you.* That is good news. You can be holy. You can be righteous. But you will never manage it. God can manage it in you. That is the good news of the gospel. The gospel is not a gospel of the love of God, it is a gospel of the righteousness of God. Neither Jesus nor the apostles ever preached the love of God to sinners. *They preached the righteousness of God*, and every statement about the love of God in your New Testament is made to those who are already redeemed and forgiven by God. It is a pearl we should not throw before swine. Our gospel is not the gospel of the love of God, it is the gospel of the righteousness of God: that God is righteous and can make you righteous, if you let him. That is good news.

Now, what happened to the multitude of the Jews? They were sold on self-righteousness. This is why few

Jews and so many Gentiles found it easier to accept the gospel: because Gentiles do not try to be righteous. It is those who have given up trying to be, and feel they never can be, who respond to the gospel. That is why Jesus found the Pharisees an impossible congregation, but the prostitutes and the men in the protection racket — tax collectors — came rushing to Jesus. Bad people welcome the gospel. Good people do not. I will tell you why: because the hardest thing in the world is to let go and repent of *your* righteousness. And that is essential if you are to get the righteousness of God. Some people think it is a case of do it yourself as far as you can, and then let him forgive the rest. No, it is all or nothing. You either try and be righteous yourself, or you let him make you righteous. There is no other choice. People know they should repent of their sins and their bad deeds, but I am amazed how many people in Christian churches do not know they have got to repent of their good deeds, their self-righteousness.

I work among gypsies a lot. There are whole camps I go to that are now totally Christian. Some of them told me they used to be bad people, cheats and thieves — and they are now honest. Their faces are open and frank. When you know you were bad it is easier to repent.

I speak in top security prisons, among people in for life, murderers, drug pedlars, and many of them welcome the gospel. They know they are bad. And

143

so they know they will never be righteous, and they welcome a gospel that says you can be righteous because God can do it in you. Repenting of your good deeds is the hardest thing in life, and the better the life you live the harder it is for you to accept the gospel of God's righteousness.

Do you really understand what I am saying? You are going to be shocked by the language I use now, but I am quoting the Bible, that is my excuse. Paul was a man who tried so hard to be righteous. And he made it, nearly — he did not manage the tenth commandment but he managed all the other nine, and a lot of laws. Do you know what he said? He used a crude Greek word, of all his righteousness; in Anglo-Saxon it is the word 'shit'. He said, *I counted shit all my righteousness*. It is like a little boy with his potty, and he has just emptied his bowels and says, 'Daddy, look what I have done.' That is how your righteousness appears to God. Isaiah, for the ladies, said something equally offensive. He said, *Your righteousness is like a used menstrual cloth*. And you do not parade that around. Now, here is crude language, but it is the New Testament and the Old Testament saying that is how self-righteousness appears to God. It disgusts him.

We are ambassadors for Christ beseeching you to be reconciled to God; him who knew no sin was made to be sin on our behalf, that we might become the righteousness of God. That is a double substitution, which I find many Christians are not very happy with. They are so happy that Jesus took our sins on him. They are not so eager to take his righteousness on themselves. But Jesus' offer in the gospel is: Give me your sins; and here is my righteousness for you. Jews stumbled because they wanted to establish their own righteousness. In the present day, I think God is allowing the troubles that are coming to Israel, until they see themselves as God sees them, and turn to him for his righteousness. When you see Orthodox Jews walking around in their old costume, one thinks: you are trying so hard to be righteous. You will not allow cars through the Mea Shearim on the Sabbath. Paul pointed out in Romans chapter ten that is the big problem that God had with the Jews: self-righteousness. So he says they pursue righteousness, they chase after it, they run after it, and they stumble over a rock in the middle of the road.

I was walking across a street in England not long ago, and I spotted a bookshop at the far side of the street. Now, my wife screams when I do that, because I have three tons of books at home! When I saw the bookshop, my eyes went straight to it and I did not see a little raised island in the middle of the road, for traffic. I was so keen to get at the books I just fell and broke my ribs. And it served me right! I was so eager to get to that bookshop I did not spot the stumbling block. That is what the Jews were doing. They were stumbling over a rock in the middle of the road as they ran after righteousness. In the book of Judges the real problem was that everybody in Israel did what was right. It was not that they were doing it wrong. They did what was right 'in their own eyes'. I find that is the biggest problem: repenting of your good deeds, your own righteousness, throwing it all away and saying I want the righteousness of God, not my own righteousness.

So Gentiles have found it easier to accept the Jewish Messiah precisely because they do not pursue righteousness. They do not try nearly as hard as the Jews to be what God wants them to be. Therefore it is much easier for them to come humbly and accept his righteousness. Mind you, there is still a bit of pride. A man said to a friend of mine, 'Do you expect me to come before God with open hands and outstretched arms and confess that I am a failure and that I cannot manage without him?' He said, 'I'm damned if I will.' My dear friend replied, 'You will be damned if you don't.' Which was a good answer. You see, it is self-righteousness that says, 'I can manage my own life, thank you. I do not need his help. I will do it myself, or kill myself in the attempt.' Paul teaches that you need to throw away all your righteousness and get a righteousness from God, but Judaism finds that very difficult, because its adherents try more than many others to be righteous before God.

Paul then reveals his heart again. All his longing, his ambition, his heart's desire is to save them. But he does not say to save 'Israel'. Now, he changes the word to 'Israelites', because he knows you cannot save a nation, you have to save them as individuals, one by one. There is no shortcut. Oh, he said, my longing is to save Israelites — which means, quite frankly, that Jews are lost and need saving. Now, I am afraid that among Christian Zionists there can arise a feeling that Jews are okay, that they are safe in God's sight, that they do not need to be evangelised. They just need to be comforted and loved and served.

Listen, the greatest need of every Jew you meet is to be saved. Those who love Israel ought to be in the forefront of evangelism of Jews, of giving them the gospel of their own Messiah, hard though it is. It is so much easier to cheer them and comfort them and 'love' them, but the real love is to save them. That was Paul's desire, and it should be ours, too. They are lost in self-righteousness and need to be saved from it and brought into the righteousness of God. And he says that it is not hard. They are making such a hard job of being righteous, whereas it is really quite easy, because the rock over which they stumble is a person, not a thing. It is a 'he' not an 'it', and his name is *Yeshua HaMashiach*. And the Jews fall over him, because they are running after righteousness and they stumble over him.

Jews were stumbling over Jesus, the rock. But Gentiles stood on the rock, finding righteousness — a righteousness that comes from above. It is not beyond, down a long road of effort, it is just up there. In fact, it is so near that Paul now says it is as near as your heart and your mouth. You do not have to climb up to heaven to reach this righteousness. You do not have to dig down into Hades, the world of the dead, to get it. It is not far away.

What does Paul mean when he says that it is in your mouth, and it is in you? He is contrasting a righteousness based on works of the law, and a righteousness that comes to you through words of faith. So simple. All it needs is a heart that believes and a mouth that confesses. Either without the other will not do it. You can believe in your heart and not confess with your mouth, and that will not do it. You can profess with your mouth and not believe it in your heart, and that will not do it. But simply believe in your heart and call on the Lord to be saved, and his righteousness is already yours. You are covered with his righteousness, and as you walk in the Spirit his righteousness will increasingly appear in your life. *He* will do it.

It is too simple for many. But more and more Gentiles seized this righteousness because it was so near and, in a sense, so simple. It is yours for the asking. *Whoever calls on the name of the Lord will be saved* says Paul, in this chapter. That is all. Believe that he is there, believe he wants to make you righteous, believe he can make you righteous, and call on him and say, 'Help me.'

Jesus helped me. I never use the 'sinner's prayer'. I do not like formulae for a start, but it is a very inadequate prayer. I always encourage a person to pray their own prayer, however simple. Call on him, speak it out, he is there.

I remember a Jewess coming to me after one meeting in Cambridgeshire. Very attractive, dark-haired, about twenty-five years of age. She said, 'Mr Pawson, are you trying to tell me that Jesus of Nazareth is still alive?'

'That is what I am saying, yes,' I replied.

She said, 'But if he is, then he must be our Messiah.' *Our* Messiah. Notice that. Not 'mine', but 'our'.

'That is true.'

'How could I find out if he is alive?' she said.

I replied, 'Very simply. I am going to leave you in this room for ten minutes, and I want you to talk to him. Just tell him about yourself.'

I came back. She knew everything. Her Old Testament came alive. She started teaching me the Bible!

I said, 'Yes, it is all true.'

She had it all there, but she had never 'called' on the name of the Lord. It is that simple. You know, it can be so simple that you miss it. And that is what was wrong. The Jews had wanted self-righteousness, and they strode after it, pursued it, and stumbled over the rock that was Christ, because he is absolutely against self-righteousness. He hates it. As we have noticed, that is why he could not get on with the Pharisees, and why prostitutes came.

I was in Winnipeg, Canada, and they put me on the local television as soon as I arrived. I said, 'Well, I am glad to be in Winnipeg because an ancestor of mine founded this city.' And even the cameraman looked at me sideways, but it is true.

Then the producer said, 'I will give you twenty minutes and you can talk about anything you like.' (I wish the BBC would do that.)

I said, 'Do you mean that?'

'Yeah. What do you want to talk about?'

'The kingdom of God.'

He replied, 'Oh. Now, this is a commercial channel and we get our income from the adverts. We've got to keep people watching. Do you think they will be interested?'

I said, 'I do not care whether they are interested or not. You said I could talk about any topic I like. I said that is my favourite topic, and it was Jesus' favourite topic.'

'Oh, alright then, go on.'

I think he thought dozens of sets would be switched off, and maybe they were. But there were telephones in the studio for viewers to call in, and after twenty minutes of talking about the kingdom of God, a telephone rang. A woman's voice said, 'Can I ask a question, for Mr Pawson?'

So I took hold of the phone and said, 'Hello. David Pawson here. How can I help?'

She replied, 'How can I get into that kingdom that you are talking about?'

'Well, tell me a bit about yourself.'

She said, 'I am a hooker, a prostitute on the street.'

I thought: I must be preaching the right gospel at last. When a prostitute wants to seize the kingdom, that is the right gospel. I said, 'Why do you want to get in?'

She said, 'Because it is time I straightened myself out.'

I said, 'You will never straighten yourself out. But Jesus can.'

But can those who still pursue their own righteousness be excused, even though it is so easy to get God's righteousness? Paul deals with that as well. Maybe they have never heard the gospel. Maybe if they did hear it they did not understand it. That would excuse them, wouldn't it? But Paul says they are without excuse. He says first of all, yes, they have got to hear. Somebody has got to go and tell them about this wonderful news that Christ is the end of the law.

Now, what does that mean? Well, we know that Christ kept the law, and we also know that he revised it, making it stricter. But he also replaced it by himself. Do you realise that? When he said *But I say to you*, he was saying the law of Moses is no longer the standard by which you live. He, Jesus, is the standard — his thinking, his attitudes, his behaviour. That is now the law of Christ for you. That is what he meant. Christ is the end of the law. Not that you do not need to be good, but from now on our standard of goodness is not what Moses said but what Jesus was, and said, and did. He has replaced Moses' law. That is the end of Moses' law.

Had the Jews heard this? Well, they had to hear it, and messengers have been dispatched. Here is the logic of Paul's argument. How can they call on someone unless they believe in him? How can they believe in him unless they have heard about him? How can they hear unless someone preaches? And how can someone preach unless they have been sent? That is a lovely argument. All the steps in how God brings his righteousness to people are there. He sends a preacher. The preacher tells people, announces it, proclaims it. Good news: you can be righteous. That is the essential good news of the gospel. Not: you need *not* be; but you *can* be. Too many evangelists and preachers today are preaching a 'gospel' that we need *not* be holy. But you know, the old hymn *There is a green hill far away* says that, 'He died that we might be forgiven, he died to make us good, that we might go at last to heaven, saved by his precious blood.' The modern version of that would be: he died that we might be forgiven, not *needing* to be good . . . . That is not the gospel. Jesus died to make us holy. He died to make us good. He died that he might take our sins and substitute his righteousness for our sins. That is the whole gospel. Paul taught that Jews know about Jesus. They have heard. And now the gospel has gone through all the earth. Well, perhaps when they heard it they did not understand it? Paul pointed out that simple Gentiles, who had no preparation, understood it perfectly. And the Jewish people had centuries of preparation.

Letting go of your goodness can be the hardest thing to do, but if you are really bad, then it is the easiest thing to do. Maybe that is why I do not often hear prayers for God's mercy in church. I hear prayers for his guidance, for security, for his provision, for our safety, for our health, and for so much else. I rarely hear someone ask, 'God, have mercy on me.' Why? We think we are not bad enough. It is people who feel they do not deserve anything who ask God for mercy. That is why it is so much easier for bad people than good people. Paul makes it clear that Jews heard and understood. And he proves that from their own scriptures, in Deuteronomy and Isaiah again. So what is the reason? It is not that they have not had a chance. They have had a choice, and they have made the wrong choice. That is Paul's analysis of the situation of his fellow countrymen. They did not choose to accept Jesus, who came offering the righteousness of God but would not accept self-righteousness. They rejected it, as many do. Paul shows that they were unwilling to submit, to obey. They were stubborn. They were obstinate. They were unwilling to go with God when he approached them through the person of his Son.

Again Paul appeals to their own scriptures. He says to them that this had been their attitude to God throughout their history. For four thousand years God has held out his hands to the Jews, and the vast majority of them have rebelled and resisted, refused the revelation of a different way to be God's righteous people on earth.

Now, if Paul ended at the end of Romans chapter ten, you could understand people coming to the conclusion that God has replaced the Jewish people with Gentiles. You could say: Well, Paul, my conclusion is that the majority of Jews have had their chance, they have missed it, deliberately; they have rejected it, and so God has rejected them. It stands to reason; it makes sense. *We* are the replacement. *We* are now the new Israel. We Gentile believers are the true Israel of God, even though we may have a scattering of Jews among us. That would have made sense, but Paul did not stop at Romans chapter ten.

IN THE FUTURE, ALL ISRAEL WILL BE SAVED

We will now look at Romans chapter eleven, where there is a completely different picture. Paul knows what his readers will be concluding from the previous two chapters. He is very clever when he argues. He has actually gone along with them so far. In effect he is saying: you are right. They must be thinking that he is now going to say God has rejected the Jews. He anticipates what they are thinking. You think God has rejected the Jews? Never! Now he tells them: because you are ignorant of their future in God's purposes. They were selected in the past, in the present they are stubborn, but in the future all Israel will be saved!

That changes the whole picture, and that deals with Gentile arrogance, and it deals with replacement theology, and it deals with anti-Semitism in the church. But can you see how skilfully Paul has led up to it? He has gone along with them. They were right as far as the present was concerned, but they are wrong about the future.

Paul did not write a letter and divide it into chapters and verses. Would you? This is a letter we are reading. Nevertheless, it is useful or convenient to refer to the chapters, and nine, ten and eleven are like a sandwich: nine and eleven have a lot in common, and ten is quite different — the filling in the sandwich. In chapter eleven we return to the themes of chapter nine. We go back to the sovereignty of God and the mercy of God; we go back to the patriarchs; we go back to a number of the themes that were picked up in chapter nine. Even the outline or structure of the chapter is the same. The first half of each of the chapters nine and eleven is about the Israel of God, and then the second half of each chapter is about the God of Israel; the focus of attention is first on his people and then on him. Chapter eleven is the climax of this section, 9–11. It is also the climax of chapters 1–11, and finishes with the doxology, just as Ephesians chapter three finishes with a doxology. But it is also the climax of the whole letter.

We have at last reached the reason why Paul wrote the letter to the Romans. He has been building up so carefully and so wisely, to the point where he now tackles the problem head on. The problem is Gentile arrogance, and the downside of that: their contempt for the Jews, both believing and unbelieving Jews — the seeds of anti-Semitism and replacement theology. This is Paul's primary concern. Now, if he had finished at the end of chapter ten, replacement theology would be the right conclusion. He has said in chapter nine, *Not all Jews are Israel*, and that, I know, shakes many, and has raised huge questions, but it is in the scripture and you need, therefore, to take that into your thinking. And if Paul had stopped at the end of chapter ten, we really are on the wrong track. Who is Israel? —that is the big question. If chapter nine says that not all

Jews are Israel, chapter ten says most of the Jews have rejected their Messiah, have refused the righteousness of God and the gospel, even though they have heard it and understood it. So have we Gentiles not replaced them? Is the church not the new Israel? Has God not finished with most of the Jews? There may be a tiny minority of them who have believed in Jesus, but it is a tiny number compared to the whole, only a few thousand out of maybe eighteen million. So chapters nine and ten might seem to suggest that the Jews are God's 'has-been' people and he is now dealing with us rather than them. But Paul did not finish there! As we have noted, it is almost as if he is supporting the Gentile believers in their thinking, right up to this point, and now he is going to devastate it. He has really got their ear.

Regrettably, the church has largely ignored chapter eleven and stopped in their thinking at chapter ten, and assumed that the present situation is permanent, that most of the Jews are out of the picture, that most of the Jews are not Israel. Only a few believing Jews are Israel. Asked 'Who is Israel?' one commentator rightly replied, 'The Jews who believe in Jesus.' True Israel, God's Israel, are the little minority of believing Jews. What the church has done, by stopping at chapter ten in its thinking, is to pull up its Jewish roots, and very early on the church decided to ignore the Jewish calendar and have its own Christian calendar, and separate Easter from Passover, and Whit Sunday from Pentecost and, worst of all, to celebrate Christ's coming at the winter festival of December 25th instead of the Feast of Tabernacles which, of course, is when Jesus was born, according to our Bible. The church pulled up its Jewish roots, but it had a problem: it kept the Old Testament. In fact, for quite a long time the early church did not have the New Testament, for it was not even written. The only scriptures they had were the Old, so what did the church do with the Old Testament and all the promises and prophecies to Israel? Well, the church took them, but it stole all the promises of blessing but none of the promises of cursing! When they took the promises of blessing, they spiritualised them, turning them into spiritual instead of physical blessings, and never took them literally.

So the church has kept the Jewish scriptures but changed them, selected them, and altogether distorted them. Some editions of the King James Version have even put headlines in the prophetic books of the Old Testament: if a blessing to Israel was promised, the headline was 'Blessing for the Church'. If it promised a curse on Israel the headline was 'Curses on Israel'. If the church had only read and studied Romans eleven, they would never have done that sort of thing. So we have to minister to a church that has pulled up its roots and is rootless, and needs to be told how to put those roots down again.

Throughout this chapter Paul is very clearly addressing only the Gentile believers in Rome. There were now Jewish believers like Aquila and Priscilla who had come back, but three times in this chapter Paul says: I am talking to you Gentile believers. 'You' is emphatic, all the way through. I am talking to you. And I am rebuking you for your arrogance that you think that you are better than the Jews. The arrogance, Paul says, was due to their ignorance about them. Arrogance is usually due to ignorance about others. If you think you are better than someone else, it is probably because you do not know everything about that person. You do not know the whole story. You think someone is an irritable, cantankerous old person; and it is probably because they have suffered greatly and you did not know. If you think you are better than others, you do not know the whole story about them. That is the way Paul tackles the problem.

A simple summary of Paul's message in the chapter would be: you are judging the Jews on their past and their present, and you are totally ignorant about their future. That is the cause of your arrogance.

When Paul looks at the Israel of God in the first part of the chapter, he answers four crucial questions, and these are the big questions that all Christians, including replacement theologians, need to look at. Firstly, have the Jews been rejected? Secondly, can they be recovered? Thirdly, have they been replaced? Fourthly, will they be restored? Your answers to those four questions will determine your attitude to the Jewish people, whether they are believers or unbelievers, but mainly your attitude to *unbelieving* Jews will be determined by your answers.

Paul knows the mind of Gentile believers, and he assumes that what he has said already will convince them that God has rejected Israel. When he says that not all Jews are Israel, and most of them have rejected the gospel, it seems to be the logical and natural conclusion that God has finished with them and he is now dealing with us, and therefore we must be better than them because we have responded and they did not. He tackles that straightaway, and he says, *Have they been rejected by God? Never.* It is the strongest possible negative statement you can make in Greek (Μη γένοιτο), which means 'never let it be', or in English: unthinkable; impossible; out of the question. I just cannot find an English phrase strong enough to communicate his reaction. Has God rejected them? He has said in the chapter that they have rejected God. The normal human assumption is that that has broken the relationship between them, but the relationship between God and Israel and between God and you is not a *contract* but a *covenant*. There is a huge difference between the two. If one party reneges on the conditions of a contract, the other party may be released from their obligation under it. You have a contract with a builder to build your house for a certain price, and the plans are there. If he reneges on that contract you could be free not to pay him. If one party in a contract fails, the other is generally released from it. But with a *covenant*, if one party breaks it, the other party still has to hold on. Marriage is a covenant in God's sight. Today it has become a contract, and it is widely assumed that if one party betrays a marriage the other party is free to marry again. But Jesus, knowing and teaching that marriage is a covenant, said that whoever divorces and remarries is committing adultery. And whoever marries a divorcee is committing adultery. What is he saying? He is saying that marriage is a covenant, and even if one party breaks the covenant the other cannot. The other is not released to make a new contract. But, in our society, if I stop loving you, you can find someone else and marry them. If I break the contract, or if you do, the other party is released. That is not the truth. In God's sight, marriage is a covenant. You promise to stay loyal to that covenant, even if it is worse and not better, even if it is in sickness and not health. But you do not have to say those words in a Register Office. It is a legal contract.

Again and again, God says through scripture: I have made a covenant with you, Israel. You may break it but I never will. I went through the Bible underlining how many times God said that. It is all the way through. He knew they would break it, but he said he would not.

I think of a man in the north of England whose wife, shortly after their marriage, got into very bad ways. She was worse than unfaithful, and she picked up a sexually transmitted disease, from which she became very ill, and the friends of that Christian man said to him, 'Why don't you divorce and find yourself a good Christian wife? She is no good to you. She does not care for you.'

He replied: 'Never. Never speak to me like that about my wife. She is my wife and I shall love her as long as there is breath in her body.' And he did. And she died, with his hands spread over her in love. That is a covenant. That is true marriage in God's sight. However badly the other behaves, the other party to a covenant stays faithful.

Now, that is a revolution in modern thinking. Say that to a Christian congregation today! I said it in America, and the pastor pushed me up against the wall and said, 'I am not going to let you leave this building until you retract that statement.' Because half his congregation was married and remarried after divorce, and he was on his third wife, and he was furious. But that is God's covenant love. And marriage was meant to be a covenant love. And God's attitude is: If you break it, Israel, you will not break me; I will hold on. If you only look at the Jews who have rejected God, or rather, rejected his greatest gift of his Son to them, you would think God is released from his covenant, but he is not. He has not rejected them. He never will. That is the first basic thing we need to know. Therefore, Paul is proving to his hearers that God hangs on to Jewish people. He, Paul, is the proof. He tells them how Jewish he is; that he was of the tribe of Benjamin, named after the first king of Israel, Saul, from that little tribe which had nearly disappeared but did not quite do so. He, Paul, had been hostile to the Messiah of God, had imprisoned people who believed, had thought it was a Jewish heresy; and he became an anti-Christian missionary, leaving his own country to go after Christians to imprison them.

He said that Jesus had held on to him. He could have said this about all the other twelve apostles. He was the thirteenth, of course, but the other twelve were all Jews too; and, of course, Jesus himself was Jewish. God held on to a remnant all the time. There never was a time when God did not have his Israel. It got very small at times, but the real Israel of God, who trusted and obeyed, found that the God of Israel was there.

There was a time when even one prophet thought they were about to die out. Elijah, says Paul, thought the Israel of God was down to one. He had said: I, even I, am the only one left of the true Israel, and they are seeking my life. You are about to lose the last one, Lord. Elijah was shown now that his human arithmetic was a little faulty. God had held on to seven thousand. Now, it was only a small minority out of maybe a million by then, but God had held on to his remnant. That means not that he forced them to stay faithful but that he gave them extra grace to which they responded. So they were fortified and favoured by grace.

I say again (against Calvinism) that grace is not an irresistible force, it is an undeserved favour, and what people make of it is their responsibility. But God had given extra grace and help to that minority to remain faithful when the whole of Israel was running after Baal, a pagan deity. Paul makes it clear that it was still the case. Paul was part of the believing remnant and for two thousand years there has never been a year in which there has not been a remnant of Jews who believed in their own Messiah, all the way through. It is a growing group today, numbered in thousands. In America, Israel and England there are a number of Messianic assemblies. I was very touched when a new Messianic assembly in London asked, 'David, would you be one of our elders?'

I said, 'But I am not Jewish, as far as I know. Why do you want me?'

They answered, 'Because we want to be one new man in Christ. We do not want to be exclusively Jewish. We would like a Gentile elder.' I was not able to do what they wanted, but I was so thrilled.

The remnant that God has always held are the Israel of God, so what about the rest, who rejected their Messiah? What has God done to them? He has not rejected them. What he has done is harden them. What he did to Pharaoh he has done to unbelieving Jews. That is why Paul talked about hardening Pharaoh in chapter nine. He says, 'God can harden whom he hardens.' That is his right. And then he went on to explain that he only does that to those who have already hardened themselves against him.

God began to do that through Isaiah, the prophet. Isaiah was called, and every time I hear preachers read Isaiah chapter six I get so frustrated. They always stop halfway through, with the words, 'Here am I, send me!' Isaiah went to the temple and had an extraordinary experience. His lips were burned. People think it is all spiritual. No, it happened, literally.

Then one of the seraphs flew to me with a live coal in his hand, which he had taken with tongs from the altar. With it he touched my mouth and said, "See, this has touched your lips; your guilt is taken away and your sin atoned for."

Then I heard the voice of the Lord saying, "Whom shall I send? And who will go for us?"

And I said, "Here am I. Send me!"

He said, "Go and tell this people:

"'Be ever hearing, but never understanding;
be ever seeing, but never perceiving.'
Make the heart of this people calloused;
make their ears dull

> *and close their eyes.*
> *Otherwise they might see with their eyes,*
> *hear with their ears,*
> *and turn and be healed."*
>
> Isaiah 6:6ff., *NIV*

So Isaiah was told to spend a lifetime doing preaching that would make people harder, more resistant, and none of them would convert. What a ministry to be called to! And there he stood, with his scarred lips, speaking through those scars, and telling them things that simply made them more resistant, harder. Jesus quoted that very verse four times in his ministry.

Jesus' parables were not to illustrate the truth and make it plain to people. They were to hide the truth and make the Jewish people harder. You have to come to terms with those words of Jesus:

> ". . . *to others I speak in parables, so that,*
> *"'though seeing, they may not see;*
> *though hearing, they may not understand.'"*
>
> See Luke 8:10

It was part of a hardening process of God. The parables of the kingdom hardened the Jews further, and Paul quoted that, because he found when he preached in the synagogues it had the opposite effect to what you might expect. It made them more resistant.

God has been in all this. When the Jews hardened their hearts against God, he helped them to harden. He did this through Isaiah, through Jesus, and through Paul. The people became more and more resistant. The word used for 'hardened' is 'calloused'. When I worked on a farm (I was going to be a farmer), my skin became calloused with hard work. It became less sensitive, harder, and it could not feel things so readily. It became more impervious to rain. This happens to your feet if your shoes do not fit properly. So callouses are hard bits of people that become insensitive and impervious, and we learn from scripture that God calloused or hardened the rest of the Jews. They became even harder than Gentiles because God hardened them. Therefore, quoting Old Testament scriptures, Paul says they are stupefied in their thinking, they cannot receive what you say, it is as if it just does not sink in, their minds are calloused, and they stumble around trying to find answers to their problems. What a description!

So God is still dealing with all Jews. Some of them, he is holding as a remnant, the true Israel of God, and the rest of them he is hardening, but he is still using them, and there are two conclusions you must not come to: firstly you must not conclude that God cannot still use them; nor, secondly, must you ever conclude that God cannot change them—because God is God. Then how did he use the hardened Jews? Paul says that if the Jews were not hard, you Gentiles would not have received the gospel so quickly. So you ought to be thankful that God hardened them because, time and again (three times it is recorded in Acts, and it must have happened many more times than that), Paul tried to reach the Jews with the gospel. First, he said: I go first to the Jew. It is theirs first. Then they hardened, their hardness rejects it, and he said, again and again, 'I turned to the Gentiles.' If you will not have me, they can. That spread the gospel to the Gentile world far more quickly than if the Jews had been responsive. Paul is saying that you ought to be thankful, God has used the 'hardened' remainder of the Jews to get the gospel more quickly to the Gentiles. That is an amazing way of thinking, isn't it? It would never have occurred to you, perhaps, unless Paul had pointed it out. God has not rejected the Jews. If they will not be used in one way he will use them in another. That is the message. God is God, and he promised to use them as a light to the nations and to bless all the families of the earth, and if they refuse the blessing, that just speeds it up for everybody else.

Our thinking already is beginning to say: Who would have thought that out? Only God — as Paul makes clear at the end of the chapter. He has not disowned all Jews, but he is using some in one way and the majority in quite a different way, to further his purposes.

But is this the permanent situation — that some Jews are the Israel of God and the rest he uses in quite a different way? That raises a second question. From now on in the passage, Paul is concentrating exclusively on the unbelieving majority, and what God's plans for them are. So the question comes: can they be recovered? Have they fallen fatally? Are they beyond redemption? Have they stumbled over the rock that is Christ and cannot get up? Do you know Paul's answer? Never! For the second time he comes out with this indignant 'Never let it be!' Unthinkable! God can still do something with them — positively, as well as negatively. Is the ratio of the true Israel to the fleshly Israel fixed, permanent? Never!

Again, we are focussed on the wrong thing. We are focussed on the *people* of Israel and not the *God* of Israel. The fact is, first, he says, many of them will convert in the future. Many! They are called to bless all families on earth and be a light to all the nations. They are already helping the nations by their rejection, so they are already a blessing to the world. And if they are already bringing riches to the whole world through their rejection of the Messiah, what will their acceptance be? Life from the dead! When I meet a converted Jew, I envy him, I really do. I wish I was a Jew. I would love to prove I had Jewish blood! Because as soon as they find Christ they have so much more than I had. I had to learn to think like a Jew; he does not. I had to learn the true meaning of the Old Testament; he does not. He has it all. I envy them! They have the covenants, the patriarchs, the oracles of God. They are natural branches. They belong. And when they all accept the Messiah, can you imagine what that will do for the world? Look at what they have done to the world in unbelief. Our arts, our sciences, our medicine, our entertainment world. You owe so much to the Jew. Do you use a telephone? A Jew invented it. Do you ever fly in an aeroplane? A Jew invented it. Do you eat tomatoes? A Jew did that for you. Do you get anaesthetic at the dentist? It was a Jew who did that. If you had a sexually transmitted disease, it can be cured now by a drug discovered by a Jew. All five Hollywood studios were Jewish. They have supplied 12% of the world's scientists, though they are only 0.8% of the world's population. In architecture and music, many are at the top. We owe them so much, and that is when they are in unbelief! What will happen when they find the Messiah? And Paul says that they are going to. He does not ask what their reception of the Messiah *would* mean for the world, but what *will* it mean for the world.

In a sense, this huge majority of Jews who rejected their Messiah are 'dead'. There is a spiritual deadness in them. Paul speaks of when they accept life from the dead. Immediately I read that, I thought of the father of the prodigal son who was glad when his son came home. The father said, 'This, my son, was dead. He is alive again.' That is what the heavenly Father will say when the Jews accept their Messiah. And what that will mean for the world, I just cannot imagine. They are streets ahead of us Gentiles in so many ways. They have had to be to survive. They are clever people. They are brilliant people. They are shrewd people. They know how to climb out of a hole. They know how to build life up again after it has been destroyed. They are wonderful people, though most are 'dead' to Jesus. But when they receive — wow! Some are already transferring from the majority to the minority. A trickle, even a stream, it is not a river or a flood yet, but it is already happening: some are coming to faith in their own Messiah. It is so exciting to find an Orthodox Jew who did not have a Christian missionary to tell him anything, but who came to Christ and belongs to the Israel of God!

It is possible to save some now, and that is Paul's longing. We do not need to wait for this big resurrection of the dead nation. I emphasise that, because some Christian Zionists have developed a heresy called 'double covenant'. Have you heard of this? The Jews are saved through their covenant, the old one, and Christians are saved through the new one. So the Jews do not need to be saved; that is heresy. It is a Christian version of a much wider relativism that says you are saved through 'sincerity' no matter what your faith may be. That is the kind of thinking that is creeping into Christian circles today. But the scripture teaches us that a majority of Jews are not saved, they are dying and facing a Christless eternity.

Like Paul, we ought to have as our top ambition to save some, if we can. So the question is, how are we going to do that? And we have so many answers: love them, serve them, do this for them, do that for them. But how are we going to do it? I want to say that all those things have their place — apologising to them for Christian anti-Semitism, repatriating them from Russia. All that is an expression of Christian love, but Paul says there is one thing that will do it, and it is none of those. They may prepare the way, but they will not do the trick, however much we long for it to happen. The one thing that will do it is to *make them jealous*.

Now, I want to draw a very careful distinction between envy and jealousy. Envy is a bad thing, but jealousy is a good thing. God is jealous, but he is not envious. Why should he be? The cattle on a thousand hills are his already. All the silver and the gold is his. God does not envy anyone, because he has everything he wants. But he is jealous. He is a jealous God. What is the difference? If I met another couple and fancied the wife more than my own wife (which I have not yet done) then I might envy the man his wife. But if someone ran off with my wife, I would be jealous. Do you see the difference? Envy is wanting what someone else has that I do not have. Being jealous is being jealous of something that is mine that somebody else has got. Never get the idea that we must make the Jews envious of what we have. Make them jealous for what is theirs! Do not talk about 'my Saviour', talk about 'your Saviour' to them: *your* Messiah. A friend of mine went into a shop, noticed the Jewish name outside, and said, 'You are a Jew?' The man in the shop said, 'Yes', very defensively. And my friend just said, 'Do you know, it was a Jew who saved my life? I will always be grateful to you Jews. I owe everything to a Jew.' 'Oh, very interesting,' the man said. 'Who was that? Would I know him?' Open door! 'Your Messiah.'

Make them jealous. 'We Gentiles have discovered what is yours.' Make them jealous, for *their* scriptures, *their* Saviour, *their* Messiah. It is all theirs, and we just came along and found it. But it is all Jewish. Now, Paul teaches: if you can somehow make them jealous for what is *theirs*; that *they* should have. Have you got the picture? He says that is the point where they will open up. Well, I must take Paul's word for it. When they resent you having what is really theirs, that is their 'resurrection'. Verse 16 is a typical rabbinical link in an argument. It looks back to what has already gone and looks forward to what he is going to say. It is the Jewish principle, based on the law of Moses, that if part of anything is holy the rest must be. Think of that as applied to the Jews. If part of Israel is holy, then the rest must be. If part of a lump of dough is holy, the rest is. This is a very important principle. You cannot think a bit of something is holy and the rest not. It is either all holy or none of it is.

With that little link, Paul comes to the third question, and here we reach the climax of his argument: are the Jews being replaced? This was the heart of the problem in the church at Rome — that the Gentiles thought they were, and that we Gentiles have now replaced the Jews. The church is now the Gentile church and is the true Israel of God. That leads to a 'superiority complex' in the Gentiles, doesn't it? We must be better. Why would God kick them out and put us in their place unless we are better than they are?

Paul really wants to treat the matter very carefully, in a balanced way, and his answer is not 'never', his answer is: *partly*, not wholly. Look at the actual facts. First, Jews have been cut out. There is no question about this: Jewish branches were not 'pruned' but have been chopped off (that is the word) their own olive tree. And the reason why they were chopped off was because even after being redeemed as God's people, they fell into unbelief.

You see, faith has to be continuous if it is to be real and to save people. One step of faith does not save you for eternity. A *life* of faith does. It is not the faith you start with, it is the faith that you finish with that saves you. When the word '*believe*' is used in the New Testament, it is used in the present continuous tense, which is not easy to translate into English from the

Greek. It is to *go on* doing something; not to do it *once* but to go on doing it. So Jesus did not say, 'Ask and you will receive, seek and you will find, knock and it will be opened,' he said: *"Go on asking and you will receive, go on seeking and you will find, go on knocking and it will be opened to you."* John 3:16 ought to be translated (check up with anybody who knows Greek): *"For God so loved the world that he gave his only begotten Son, that whoever goes on believing in him will not perish but go on having eternal life."* Has that changed that verse for you? It does not say whoever has once believed has eternal life. It says whoever is believing, whoever goes on believing. It is not *believed*, it is *believes*. Whoever is *going on believing* has not been given eternal life as a package; he goes on having it, therefore the moment he stops believing he is in danger of losing eternal life. Or as Jesus put it more clearly: *"I am the true vine. . ."*; *"Abide in me. . ."*; and, *"If anyone does not remain in me, he is like a branch that is thrown away and withers; such branches are picked up, thrown into the fire and burned."*

Well, what does that mean? It means that the branch never has life in itself. It only has life by abiding in the vine, which is why John's Gospel also says, *We have this life in his Son.* You do not have it in yourself. You have eternal life in him, and while you remain in him you go on having eternal life, because the life, the sap of the tree, keeps coming into the branch. If the branch is cut off from the vine or the tree, it is dead, and is burned. I underline this because the most damaging phrase in Christian circles today is 'once saved, always saved', a phrase you will not find in scripture. We will return to that in a moment.

Some Jews were cut out because they drifted into unbelief after being redeemed from Egypt. And that is how you get cut out of the olive tree. Gentiles were grafted in, in their place. But notice the word 'some'. Some Jewish branches were chopped out, and Gentile branches were grafted in 'among the others'. Not all the Jewish branches were cut off. The olive tree still has, and always will have, Jewish branches in it, and the Gentile branches (we 'wild olives', and we were wild in more ways than one) have been grafted in among the Jewish branches. That is what Paul teaches. There has been only a partial replacement and it is only of the branches. The tree trunk is still there, the roots are still there, and the Jewish branches are still there. Stop thinking about replacement! It is only a *partial* replacement of *some* of the branches. Do not get the idea there is a new tree. Do you understand what Paul is saying? So when people ask, 'Have Gentiles replaced the Jews as God's people?' I say: only some of them.

Then Paul approaches it from a different angle. He says not only that this is the actual result, that some wild olive branches are being grafted in, even though they do not really fit, among the other Jewish branches in a Jewish tree trunk with Jewish roots, but that even that situation can reverse. He said, first, that Gentile branches can be cut out again. Now hear this, especially if you are a 'once saved, always saved' person: Gentile branches can be cut out again, because it is the same God dealing with us, and he cuts out those who fall into unbelief. Paul says that you are only in there because of faith, but if you lose that, if you drift from it, you too will be cut off if you do not continue in the kindness of God. That passage alone would tell me that 'once saved, always saved' is wrong. But it is not the only relevant passage. I have written a book entitled *Once Saved, Always Saved?* and I have gone through eighty passages of the New Testament that say the same thing as this one: you can be cut out. Continue in God's kindness, or you too, like those Jewish branches, will be cut out. Furthermore, Jewish branches could be grafted in, in your place. Indeed, it is much easier for God to get a Jew grafted in than a wild Gentile, because they fit. And when a Jew comes to Christ, I am astonished how quickly they fit. They just have it all. It is their tree and their roots. It was not my roots. I was a wild olive, but I have been grafted in, in the place of a Jewish branch. But I could be cut off, as they were, and a Jewish branch could be grafted in where I am. That should keep you humble, Paul teaches: You Gentiles boasting that you have replaced Jewish branches! You could be cut out and they could be grafted back in.

Now Paul has prepared the way for the biggest revelation of all. Not only could they easily be grafted back in, they *will* be. We come to the fourth question: Will they be restored? And the most surprising statement in the letter, which he has hinted at already, concerns what their reception will mean: life from the dead. Now he comes right out with it, saying, *I am going to tell you a mystery* — because you are so arrogant towards the Jewish people. That word 'mystery' is often misunderstood by Christians. It does not mean something mysterious; it does not mean something you cannot grasp or cannot understand. It means quite simply: it has been a secret up to now; it has been one of God's hidden secrets that now he is telling. It is not a mysterious mystery, it is something that nobody could have possibly guessed with their reason, but now they can understand it with their reason. It is a plain, simple statement that one day all Israel will be saved. Now, you can understand that, can't you? It is straightforward, and yet there has been so much debate and discussion about the meaning of this mystery, and the replacement theology teachers fight very hard to give a different interpretation.

That statement to me is clear. *Some* are being saved now, but one day *all Israel* will be saved. We need to give careful attention to this, because here is the key verse, the interpretation of which really affects your whole attitude to the Jewish people.

Let us look at what I think is the wrong interpretation of the verse first. What do the replacement theologians make of this verse? It would be good to look at the context now: *I do not want you to be ignorant of this mystery, brothers, so that you may not be conceited: Israel has experienced a hardening in part until the full number of the Gentiles has come in* (Romans 11:25, *NIV*).

The hardening of the majority of Jews is only temporary; it is only for a time, not for ever; and one day it will be removed, and *so* all Israel will be saved. But in between, Paul tells us *when* this will happen: when the last Gentiles have been grafted in.

That is all straightforward. Now see how the replacement theologians deal with it. This gets a bit technical now, but I think you need to know this so that you can argue it with them. They build everything on the word 'so'. A little word of two letters in English. *And so all Israel will be saved*. The word being translated 'so' means 'thus'. It does not mean 'then'. They say that Zionists are translating it 'and then all Israel will be saved', after all the Gentiles are in. They say no, it says, 'when all the Gentiles are brought in, so all Israel will be saved.' And they say 'so' means that that is the result of what has just been mentioned. They argue: when all the Gentiles are in, so all Israel will be saved, meaning the church *is* Israel, and the completion of the Gentile church will be all Israel saved.

They say: Zionists change the word 'so' meaning 'thus' to the word 'then', as something else. But they say it is all the Gentiles being brought in that makes all Israel saved: God's Israel, the church, the new Israel.

This is a very important point, which I must come back to. Therefore in the phrase *so all Israel will be saved*, that supposedly means: 'so all the Gentile church will be saved'. It may include a few converted Jews, but it is the Gentile Israel that is being referred to here. It is the whole Gentile church that is being saved. Now that would simply mean that when all the Gentiles are in, the church, the new Israel, is complete and the job of mission is over. I hope I have made that clear enough; but I hope you do not agree with it, and I hope you understand that that is the argument which the majority of churches in my country use to criticise those of us who take a different meaning.

Now let me come to what I believe is the right interpretation, word by word. Let us take that word 'Israel' first. *And so all Israel will be saved*. 'Israel' cannot mean the church because it is used throughout the New Testament always as referring to the Jewish people. It is used seventy-two times in the New Testament, and not once does it refer to Gentiles. That word is always Jewish in the New Testament. The only possible exception is the one the church seizes on, where Paul says at the end of Galatians chapter six, *Peace be to all who follow this rule, even to the Israel of God*. But actually, that is a mistranslation. The word is *and* the Israel of God. *To all the Christians and the Israel of God*. But it has been changed in your Bible to *even* the Israel of God, and they built everything on that one ambiguous text. But in every other case in the New Testament, 'Israel' means 'Jews'. And throughout chapters nine to eleven, the word 'Israel' is always used elsewhere of Jews. Why would Paul suddenly change it? Even more striking, not only is the word 'Israel' always Jewish in the whole New Testament, and it is always Jewish in the rest of chapters nine to eleven, but even in this same sentence 'Israel' clearly means Jews. Israel has been hardened in part. Is that the Christian church? Of course not. It is the Jews. Nobody is going to claim that the church has been hardened. And that is in the same sentence. So people are wanting us to believe that the name 'Israel' has changed its meaning from the beginning of the sentence to the end. I am sorry, but that is crazy. The same word in the same context in the same sentence means the same thing. That is a principle of Bible study.

Now, let us take another word, 'saved'. Here let me say something to Christian Zionists. This does not mean saved from the terrorists. It does not mean saved politically, saved economically or saved in any other way, it means saved from sin. And Paul has used that word all the way through. He says he longs to save some. What does he mean? To give them political peace? No, I tell you now, we must always remember that their greatest need for peace is peace with God. It really is. Never lose sight of that. We can get so absorbed in praying for the peace of Jerusalem politically that we forget that the need of most inhabitants of Jerusalem is peace with God through Jesus Christ our Lord. They need to be saved from sin, and as we shall see in the next verse, from the godlessness of Jacob. I once said something on Israeli television about the 'godlessness' of Israel, and the interviewer asked me, 'What do you mean, godless? Do you mean that we must all become like Orthodox Jews?' And it slipped out before I could control myself, but it was, I believe, the truth. I said, 'The Orthodox Jews are as godless as the secular Jews. They need God just as much.' And she said, 'We have got a headline.'

So, there we are. Saved from sin by grace through faith. That is what Paul means when he says 'All Israel will be saved'. He never meant anything else but spiritual salvation from sin and godlessness. Because you can be terribly religious and still be godless, did you know that? You can be without God even in the middle of religion. It is *peace with God* that is needed, and one day they will have it.

Now, let us take the next phrase: 'will be'. That in itself shows that this phrase is not the church, because when the church is completed it has been saved, all the way through. As Gentiles come in they are saved. But the tense of the verb *saved* here is future. They *will* be. It does not make sense to say when all the Gentiles are in, the church will be saved, they will already have been saved. But Israel is not. Let us take now that crucial little word 'so' in *And so all Israel will be saved*. The replacement theologians say when all the Gentiles are in, *and so* the result is that all Israel has been saved, or will have been saved. But that is to make a fundamental mistake. The 'and so' refers to what has been said before it. But you must take the whole sentence of what is said before it, and 'when all the Gentiles are in' is not the main clause of the sentence. It is a secondary clause, simply saying *when* this will happen. The 'and so' refers to the main sentence, which is: the hardening will be removed from Israel. The hardening is only until the Gentiles are all in . . . *and so all Israel will be saved*. The hardened ones will lose their hardening. That is what 'so' refers to. It is not referring to all the Gentiles coming in. That is only *when* it happens. It is referring to the day when God takes the hardening away and makes them sensitive and open. Do you see that? They just have not taken the word 'so' back far enough to the main sentence. They have taken it back to a secondary clause that is only there to describe when the hardening will be removed, but the 'so' is the result of the hardening of the heart taken away. Now, does that not make more sense?

Finally, I must take the little word 'all' and ask what

that really means. Israel must mean Jews. 'Saved' is future tense. 'So' refers to the removal of the hardening. But who is 'all'? There are four possibilities, and I am not going to be dogmatic, I will leave you to choose. I will tell you which I think.

First, some Christian Zionists have wrongly assumed that 'all Israel' means *all Jews who have ever lived*, in which case, frankly, there is no need to evangelise them. You see how that immediately affects your attitude. The Jews, I can support them, I can love them, I can comfort them, but I do not need to save them because they are going to be saved anyway. I do not believe Paul meant that. If he did, it would mean that Jews are the only nation you do not need to evangelise.

The second possibility is *all Jews who are alive when it happens*. It could mean that. If Christian Zionists believe that we are in the last, last days and any day now they are all going to be saved, why bother to evangelise them, which only offends them? But who says we are in the last, last days? I do not know. There are still at least twenty signs to be seen before Jesus gets back, and I do not see them yet. They could come quickly. We must never think because Israel are all going to be saved that they do not need to be saved now. So, that interpretation of *all Israel*, as signifying 'all Jews who have ever lived', I believe is not the true meaning.

But there is a third possibility that I want to put

before you. Paul is steeped in the Old Testament. He has been quoting it (nearly forty times in these few chapters) and the phrase 'all Israel' is very common in the Old Testament. When you find a phrase from the Old Testament in the New, you ask what does it mean in the Old, and it does *not* mean every Jew who is alive. Let me go back to the story of David. When David became king he was in Hebron, his capital —not in Jerusalem, that came later. And it says *all Israel* came to David. That did not mean every man, woman and child. Hebron would not have been big enough. It would have been hundreds of thousands if it meant every Jew alive. It did not, because in the next chapter it says all the twelve tribes came to David at Hebron. So 'all Israel' meant all twelve tribes. And in the next chapter it says all the elders of Israel gathered to David.

So we know that all Israel did not mean every man, woman and child, it meant representatives of the whole nation, elders from every tribe. And that is the way the phrase 'all Israel' is used all the way through the Old Testament. 'All Israel' gathers for the feast in Jerusalem, but that does not mean 'everybody', it meant that from every part of Israel representatives gathered, as representing the whole nation. So it may be that this phrase means a final large group representing the whole nation. That would tie up with Revelation chapter seven. Do you remember that twelve thousand from each of the twelve tribes are protected by God during the great tribulation? I just mention that; I am going to wait and see. What is absolutely clear is that it will be a huge number, possibly the majority representing all twelve tribes.

So I will translate it tentatively as *Israel as a whole*. That is my paraphrase, if you like. As to whether it means all who were alive at that time or a representative group of the whole nation, I am just going to wait and see, and I will tell you after it has happened whether you were right or wrong! But what it does mean is a large group, in utter contrast to the trickle at the moment; it will be Israel as a whole.

So in chapter nine Paul says, *Not all Israel are Israel*, meaning: not all the physical Israel is God's spiritual Israel. Can you see what this means? There is the *fleshly* Israel, and there is the *faith* Israel, who are circumcised in their heart as well as their body. The tension we have to live with is: which is 'Israel' today? But forget that question, and ask: what will Israel be tomorrow? The answer is that the paradox we have to live with will be resolved. The tension is that we want to support and love the whole Israel, and yet they are not all the Israel of God, but they *will* be. The tension is resolved when all Israel will be saved, then we will not have that question any more. The question is only there because at the moment, in the present, we are not quite sure which 'Israel' is Israel. God wants them all to be his

186

Israel, and one day they will be. Today the vast majority of Jews are unconverted, but God is still committed to them. He has brought them back to the land in unbelief. They are still not his 'Israel', but he is still committed to the big 'Israel', because he made the covenant with them. He made the covenant with the *fleshly* Israel, but he wanted them to be *faith* Israel, circumcised in their hearts as well as their bodies. One day they will be, and because we live in the future rather than the present, and are the people of tomorrow, we live in that future mystery, and therefore we ought to be able to cope with the contradiction in the present.

We live in tension. We keep asking ourselves who is Israel, because they are not all the Israel of God, yet. But they are going to be. Their potential is to be 'all Israel saved', and the Israel of God, and what will that be for the riches of the world? It is the tension between the present and the future that raises the question: who is Israel really? Just as there is a tension in the Christian life: has the kingdom come, or has it not come yet?

The answer is both. It is already present, but it has yet to be consummated. Every Christian lives in the tension between the now and the then. We groan in our bodies, waiting for the redemption of our bodies, because I am only half-saved. This old body is on its way out now and I am going to be thirty-three again one day! Paul says I am going to get a glorious body like unto his [Christ's]. Do you think that will be an old shaky man? Never. If it is like his, I will be thirty-three again, and I cannot wait to be that. In your seventies, you begin to think hard about your new body. A Christian lives in the tension between the present state and the future hope, but his real thought is in the future hope, and every Jew you see in Jerusalem potentially is a saved Jew, and that changes your attitude. How could you say God has rejected them? How could you say, 'We have replaced you'? Be careful, you could be cut out, and not only could a Jew branch be grafted in, in your place, but the whole Jewish nation is going to be grafted back into their own tree, their own trunk, their own roots, and we are living on the Jewish roots. We draw our life from the olive tree which is Israel.

I believe it is heresy to say the church is the new Israel. The church, by God's grace, is part of the old Israel now. That is the real situation. When you hear someone say 'the church is the new Israel', say, 'No, we are not, we have become part of the old Israel; part of the real Israel, the Israel of God. And by God's grace I am now a son of Abraham, and I am part of the true Israel.'

That is the real Israel, and one day all Israel will be the real one, the true one. Now, that is the balance. It is very difficult keeping that balance right. Some Christian Zionists go overboard altogether and regard the whole of the present Israel as God's Israel, willy-nilly, without qualification. It is not. But it will be.

So we cannot behave as if Gentiles have replaced the Jews. Many branches have replaced some branches, and that is all. And one day, they will be grafted back in. The contradiction that we have to live with is at the present many are enemies of the gospel, and that really hurts. Some can be hard and hostile when you tell them about their own Messiah.

I have found, however, that it is quite wrong for Christians to hide their faith in Jesus Christ when dealing with Jews. It is a mistaken fear. Many years ago I went to visit the then Chief Rabbi of a major city in Africa and sat in his study. He looked at me shrewdly, and said, 'Have you come to dialogue, or do you want to convert me?' I thought: what answer does he want to that? But I wanted to be honest, and I said, 'I would give anything for you to share my faith.' Then he said, 'Right, now we can talk. I am fed up with Christians hiding their faith and pretending to dialogue.'

I have learned this: Jewish people know you believe in Jesus. Why hide it? Share it. But it is a contradiction. There is hostility to the gospel. For your sake, their enmity has brought the gospel to you, so do not get irritated with it. But remember they are still beloved by God. For the patriarchs' sake. For Abraham, Isaac and Jacob's sake, who are not dead but still very much alive, and it is for their sake that he loves them all. Remember that. Even when they appear to be hostile to you, they are beloved to God.

Paul continues, *as far as election is concerned, they are loved on account of the patriarchs, for God's gifts and his call are irrevocable* (Romans 11:29b, *NIV*). The earth is, firstly, the Lord's, for he made it; secondarily it belongs to whoever he gives it to, and he gave the promised land to the patriarchs. His calling is also irrevocable, and his calling to them was to bless all the nations of the earth, and whether they accept the gospel or refuse it, either way they bless the nations. We owe so much to the Jews; my Bible is written by thirty-nine Jews and one Gentile, and he (Luke) got it from the Jews. My Saviour is Jewish. The apostles of the church are Jewish, and the city of the new Jerusalem, where I will one day live, by God's grace, has twenty-four names inscribed on the foundation gates, and every one of them Jewish.

God thought all this out. Oh, what a God! His plan is to have a relationship with every human being on only one basis: mercy. He will not relate to people who are self-righteous, who think they are good enough for him, who think they deserve that relationship, who think they have merit before him. He does not want to relate to people like that, he wants to relate to people who will be grateful for his mercy. That is his choice, and that is his freedom. *He does not like self-righteous people.* We say: I thank you that I am not like other men, I fast twice in the week and I give tithes for all that I possess. I was speaking in an Orthodox synagogue on the significance of the Holocaust for Jews and Christians, and when I had finished a man got up and prayed that prayer with his little cap on: 'Lord, I thank you that I am a devout Jew and that I keep your laws,' and he went on like that. It was weird, like being back in the parable of Jesus!

The man at the back of the temple had said, *"God, be merciful."* He was a tax collector, and that means he was in the protection racket, a 'Mafia' man. And Jesus said that man went down to his house justified. I do not like the word 'justification', it is much too Latin. I prefer the pidgin English translation in New Guinea: 'God, he say, I'm alright.'

I imagine that tax collector going back to his wife, and his wife saying, 'Had a good day at the office?'

'I have not been at the office, I have been in the temple.'

'What? You in the temple? Are you blackmailing the priest now?'

'No, I was praying.'

'You, praying? You have not prayed since we married, and I bet you never prayed before that.'

'Yes, I was praying.'

'And you think he heard you?'

'He did. Life is going to be different now . . . .'

Anybody who asks for mercy gets it from God. He loves to be merciful. So this is his great plan: to show mercy to the Gentile believers first, through the 'rejection' by the Jews; and to show mercy to all the Jews next, through the 'acceptance' by the Gentiles. What a plan! Nobody would have thought that up but God, because he wants to have mercy on all so he has mercy on the Gentiles because of the Jews, and on the Jews because of the Gentiles because he wants to show mercy to all mankind. What a merciful God we have, and that is his historical plan, and that is what he is going to do, and his purpose will be completely fulfilled. No wonder, then, that Paul finishes up in sheer praise of the majesty of God — not just his mercy but his majesty. He is above our intelligence, his ways and thoughts are higher than ours, the way he thinks things out in his mind and the way he puts them into practice in his method, is beyond our intelligence. This means not that we cannot understand it, but we would never have thought it up. But we can just grasp what a plan this is, to show mercy to Jews and Gentiles through each other. What an amazing plan!

Then: God is above our influence, too. Who can give him any advice? Who can tell him what to do? Who can give him counsel? Who can say, 'I've thought of a better way, God, try my way'? And who can give him any assets? You cannot bribe God. In one of my favourite texts in the Psalms, it says that if God were hungry he would not tell you. Isn't that lovely? It then goes on to say that the cattle on a thousand hills are his, and the silver and gold, but I just love that way of putting it. If I were hungry, I would not tell you. That puts me in my place.

He is above our intelligence. He is above our influence. And he is above our independence. We think we can manage without him. Rubbish! He is the Creator and every creature depends on him, whether they realise it or not.

For from him and through him and to him are all things. To him be the glory for ever. Amen.

4

ISRAEL IN HEBREWS

We simply do not know who wrote this challenging letter which the author calls *my word of exhortation* (13:22). Whenever the writer talks about himself, he uses masculine words, so it is written by some anonymous man. We do not know where it was written *from* (or where it was written *to*), but there is a little hint right at the end: *Those from Italy salute you*. And the greetings of some expatriates in other countries are being sent. We do not know much about this letter, but we do know who it was written *for*: believing Jews, 'Messianic' Jews. They were immature converts. The writer says that he has to feed them with milk when they should be feeding on meat. He has to go back to the beginning with them. The one thing we are absolutely sure about is *why* Hebrews was written: these Messianic Jews were considering going back into Judaism.

That has happened many times through the centuries. Jews who have come to faith in the Messiah,

Yeshua, have gone back into the Jewish religion. They have gone back from the church into the synagogue. There have been many reasons for this. Sometimes they have been disappointed with the church and with other Christians. Sometimes they have been Gentilised and turned into Anglicans, Baptists and Presbyterians, and no longer feel their identity as Jews. Sometimes it is due to incredible hostility from family and friends, and life has just become too uncomfortable. Sometimes it is purely a matter of culture. Why, then, are these Hebrews, who need this letter, considering going back to Judaism? The answer is very simple: for their own safety, and for the comfort and safety of their families. They are considering leaving Christianity and going back to Judaism — not to the rabbinic Judaism of today, but the biblical Judaism of two thousand years ago.

We need to know some history to understand this. Rome had many gods. The Roman empire was polytheistic and when the Romans conquered another country with another religion, their strategy was to include the god (or gods) of the conquered nation in their imperial religion. There was a huge, domed temple in Rome, which still stands, called the Pantheon (which means 'all gods'). This is where all the gods of the empire were worshipped. But this policy ran into trouble when Rome conquered the Jewish people, because the Jews flatly refused to give them a statue of Yahweh. They knew perfectly well that they had been told by God never to make a graven image, so they did not have a statue to give. Moreover, the Jews were monotheists. They believed in one God, and only one. So they would not allow their religion to be placed alongside other religions. However, the Roman authorities were kind to the Jewish people, excusing them from joining in the all-gods religion of the empire. So the Jews became what is known as a *religio licita*, a legal religion, registered, allowed to practise their own religion.

Then, of course, came Jesus the Jew. The first followers of Jesus were all Jews, and at the beginning of the story of our faith they were protected under the umbrella of Israel. They were regarded as a Jewish sect, so under that legal religion they were protected. But as soon as Gentiles began to join, as soon as they accepted Jesus as their Lord, it became obvious to the Roman authorities that this was, indeed, a new religion — that it was not the Jewish faith that had permission to practise its own religion, it was something different. Christianity became what the Roman authorities called a *religio illicita*, meaning an illegal religion, an outlawed and underground religion, that was neither accepted nor registered by the authorities. That meant persecution. It began with verbal insults, then their property began to be vandalised, then there were assaults on their persons, and even imprisonment. It was very obvious that this was heading up to martyrdom, and that Christians would pay for their faith with their lives. Now, the letter to the Hebrews mentions verbal insults, personal assaults, vandalised property, but it says, *You have not yet resisted unto blood*.

So it was because of this that these Messianic Jews were considering going back to the synagogue where they would be safe, where they would be in a legal religion. They could still be secret believers in *Yeshua*, but they would now be protected by Rome. That was the temptation: for them and their families to go back into Judaism and so be safe from all the pressures that were building up against this new religion, Christianity.

So the message to the Hebrews is very simple. The whole letter can be summed up by saying: Don't slip back, but run forward; keep going; whatever you do, don't go back. The writer of the letter uses every rhetorical device he can to persuade them not to go back. He uses very telling arguments. He uses very tender appeals. And he uses some very tough warnings. Some of the greatest warnings against backsliding are to be found in the letter to the Hebrews, and that makes it relevant to us as well.

So let us look at the three ways the writer of Hebrews tries to persuade his readers not to go back into Judaism. You can sum up all the *telling arguments* rather like this: You have found a 'better' religion, a 'better' faith. You are better off now that you believe in *Yeshua*. If you go back into Judaism you will be worse off. It is an inferior religion and an ineffective religion. It does not work. And you are much better off now because you have the Son of God. They do not. They have angels; the Old Testament is full of angels — Jacob's ladder and all that. But why go back to angels when you have the Son of God? The Son of God is better than Moses and better than Joshua, the pioneers you looked to as the founders of your nation. Angels are creatures, but the Son of God is the Creator. How much better!

In Judaism you have the temple, the sacrifices and the priests, but the sacrifices do not work. You have to keep on offering them, year after year after year. In Jesus you have the one, and the once for all, sacrifice, that is far better. You had your old priests, but in Jesus you have a High Priest who is sinless and will always be there to make intercession for you. And you want to go back to the old priests?

Now these are all very telling arguments about what you have to lose if you turn away from *Yeshua HaMashiach*! That needs to be said to every Messianic Jew. Never consider going back to that old religion.

Then the writer uses *tender appeals* to them on the grounds of his confidence in them: I have every confidence that you won't go back; I believe in you; God knows how much you have done already for him; God knows you, and I know you; and I appeal to you, please, do not go back.

Then, to these very tender appeals and telling arguments, he adds some *tough warnings*. I suppose we all know about Hebrews chapter six, in which he says if you go back you can never change your mind. There can never be repentance because you have crucified the Son of God afresh. Now, how could they have done that? The answer is very simple. Already the Jewish synagogues were beginning to disown Messianic Jews, and one of the conditions of a Jew going back to the synagogue was that they had to stand up in public and swear that they no longer believed in *Yeshua*. It was only on that condition that they could go back to the safety of the synagogue. In taking that kind of public oath, they were crucifying the Lord afresh. They were lining up with those who put him on the cross. They were disowning him. And, of course, Jesus said, *". . . whoever disowns me before men, I will disown him before my Father in heaven."*

And for that there can be no repentance, says the writer of this letter. It is not just the possibility of slipping away from Christ, but there is no possibility of getting back. That was a very serious warning. Right at the beginning of this letter, he writes: *How shall we escape if we neglect so great a salvation?* He is not talking to unbelievers, he is talking to Christians. 'How shall *we* escape, if *we* neglect . . . ?' You do not just have to turn away from Christ, but just *neglect* your salvation.

But the severest warning is in chapter ten, which many Christians do not seem to have noticed: *If we deliberately keep on sinning after we have received the knowledge of the truth, no sacrifice for sins is left, but only a fearful expectation of judgment and of raging fire that will consume the enemies of God* (10:26f., *NIV*). And: *It is a dreadful thing to fall into the hands of the living God* (v. 31, *NIV*). That is said to Christians, to Messianic Jews, to believers. These warnings are all for believers, and they tell us one very important truth, which many Christians cannot accept: you can lose your salvation. It is very clear there that the New Testament does not teach 'once saved, always saved'. Although the Messianic Jews who received this letter needed to hear that, we today need to hear it, too. If we had been able to keep everybody who has professed to believe in Christ, our churches would be packed. But my country is full of people who once went to church, who once said they believed, but who have backslidden. And this letter is a very important letter for backsliders to hear. There are no more severe warnings about losing your salvation than in the letter to the Hebrews, though there are actually eighty other passages in the New Testament warning us that we can lose what we have in Christ. So the writer says press on, look to Jesus, run the race, do not look back. Above all, he says, go to Jesus outside the camp — because Jesus was crucified outside Jerusalem, and that is a very important fact. He was rejected, and we are to go to him outside the camp. Yes, we are to be persecuted; yes, we may even have to die for our faith. Do you know how many are dying for Jesus nowadays? It is estimated that as many as 268,000 Christian believers died for their faith in just one year in the twentieth century. Thank God if you are in a country where you do not have to face death for your Lord.

So here are these young, immature Christians, Messianic Jews. They are already suffering persecution, but they are now beginning to face death, and the possibility not just of prison but of execution — and this letter is written to teach them not to go back but to press on. Well, what has all this got to do with Israel? What this letter says about two people is relevant, and the two people are Abraham and Moses. In the great chapter eleven, where you have the heroes of faith one after another, there is more space given to Abraham and Moses than any other heroes, and it is to these two people that we must now turn.

First of all, let us look at Abraham and what this letter says about him. It points to the covenant that God made with Abraham — the promise. In Hebrews chapter six we have a unique passage arguing that if God breaks a promise to Abraham you cannot trust him. God would be unreliable. You could not put your faith in any other promise of God if he went back on his promise to Abraham. God promised two things to him: (1) seed; (2) land. A people descended from him, and a place of their own to live in, for ever.

That promise was made in the most serious way. It was sealed in blood, in a sacrifice, and God swore an oath. When God swears, how does he swear? All swearing is by a power greater than yourself; you are calling on that power to kill you if you tell a lie. In an English court of law, before you can be a witness you have to put your hand on a Bible and say, 'I swear by Almighty God that I will tell the truth, the whole truth and nothing but the truth' — unless you opt to 'affirm' instead. It has become a formality, though. People do not mean it any more, but originally it meant simply, 'I call on God to kill me if I tell a lie in this court.' That is what swearing means. It is an oath to confirm your own speech by the fear of a power greater than yourself that will punish you if you do not keep that word. But how can God swear, since there is nobody above him to kill him if he does not keep his word? The answer is that he swears by himself. So he says, *"By myself I have sworn."* Chapter six of Hebrews says that covenant with Abraham was made with an oath. If God breaks that covenant, we have no hope. As believers in *Yeshua*, we could not even trust *Yeshua*'s word now. But he goes on to say that we have an anchor for the soul (he frequently uses nautical terms, talking about lowering your sails; of drifting away) — because of Abraham's covenant and the oath that accompanied it. Now, therefore, that oath still stands. That covenant still stands. The land still belongs to Abraham and his descendants.

As we noted earlier, Abraham, Isaac and Jacob are not dead, they are still alive. Jesus said that God is *"not the God of the dead, but of the living."* He is the God of Abraham, Isaac and Jacob. It is amazing to me that God would make a covenant with human beings at all, but to adopt human beings' names! When my wife married me, she had to have my name, because we had a covenant between us, and God will always be known as the God of Abraham, Isaac and Jacob. That is his name. Three human names now belong to him for ever. They are still alive; God is still alive. The covenant is still there.

Now, if all this is true, then certain things follow. First of all, to neglect the Abrahamic covenant and then try to negotiate peace is to leave out the most important factor. Secondly, any Christian who does not believe that God will keep his promise to Abraham has undermined his own faith — because no longer can he trust God to keep his word. No longer has he any guarantee that God is reliable. Yet God will never go back on his promise. It is impossible.

Those who teach replacement theology, who deny that the land still belongs to Israel, are undermining their own faith, because they are saying that God does not keep his word; that God breaks his promises. That is a serious charge.

Let us look at the other side of this. There are two sides. One is God's faithfulness to Abraham, but the other side is Abraham's faithfulness to God. Many people do not realise that in the Hebrew language of the Old Testament, and in the Greek language of the New, faith and faithfulness are the same word. You cannot have faith unless you are faithful. Standing by your faith is part of faith: going on believing. As we have already seen, in the New Testament, the word 'believe' is so often in the present continuous tense of the Greek language, which means to go on doing something.

We are told that Abraham is an example of someone who kept faith with God. And in chapter eleven, where the Old Testament saints are listed one after another, there are some wonderful statements about their faith. (We will return to that later, but it gives us two examples of Abraham's faith.) Faith is seen in what they *did*. Their faith was visible. They would not have done what they did if they did not believe. That is why James, in chapter two of his letter, writes, *Faith without works is dead*. It cannot save. Do not be put off by that word 'works', he means actions. Faith without actions is dead. It cannot save. Faith needs to *act* to be true faith.

When our three children were young we played a game called 'Faith'. They would climb up the stairs in the house, about five steps up, and stand, the three of them in a row, and I would stand at the bottom of the stairs with my hands behind my back, and they would say, 'Daddy, if we jump will you catch us?' And I used to say, 'I might, and I might not. You'll have to find out.' They loved this game, it was their equivalent of video nasties, I think, but they would stand there with their tummies turning upside down, wondering whether to jump. Then one of them would jump and I would catch them, and another would jump and I would catch them! Because they never had any guarantee that I would catch them, they had to jump, and that was their act of faith.

What did Abraham do? He did two things. One thing he did to show his faith in God was to take Isaac and go to a hill called Moriah to kill him, because God told him to. But what an act of faith that was. Do you know why? Because he set off for the journey. Isaac, who was not a boy but in his early thirties (read your Bible carefully), could easily have prevented his old dad from doing what he did. Isaac was carrying the wood. *"The fire and wood are here,"* Isaac said, *"but where is the sacrificial animal?"* They had left all the servants at the foot of the mountain, and Abraham had said to them: *"You wait here with the donkey while I and the lad go over there. We will worship and then we will come back to you."* Have you ever noticed that? *We* will come back. And we are told in the letter to the Hebrews that Abraham was convinced that God could raise the dead, which he had never done before. Abraham knew that God, if Abraham was obedient, and killed the young man, would raise him from the dead, and they would come back together. What faith, when nobody else had ever yet believed in a resurrection!

The other way Abraham expressed his faith is so relevant to us today, and it is this: he lived in a tent until he died. Now, what faith is there in that? I have seen photographs of the houses in Ur of the Chaldees where Abraham first lived. They are brick-built and they were two storeys high. So Abraham left a brick-built house at this advanced age, and he never lived in a house again. When he got to the new land he still lived in a tent, as the Bedouins do. Maybe you have seen them. Why did he do that? Because of his faith. He would not have found any bricks, nor was there mud to make them, but there were stones everywhere, and you could build some kind of a stone hut or house in a matter of a week or two. Yet he never built a house. He lived in a tent, and so did Isaac, and so did Jacob. Why? Because Abraham was homesick in this land. He never felt at home in it. And we are told in Hebrews chapter eleven he was homesick — not for Ur of the Chaldees with his comfortable brick house, he was homesick for a heavenly country, a 'better' country, where he knew he really belonged. What is a home? It is the place where you are known the best and still loved the most. 'Home' — what a lovely word it is.

Abraham never found a home in the promised land, even though God said that he was giving it to him and his descendants forever. He was not at home there; he was not even thinking of a city there — he was looking for a city whose builder and maker is God. We know it as the new Jerusalem, and it is not a city built down here, it is a city built 'up there'. It is going to come down here one day, but Abraham's home was not the promised land. He was homesick for heaven. Because Abraham was looking for the heavenly country, God was not ashamed to be his friend. That is what it says, in Hebrews chapter eleven. Read it!

Now, I have a sharp message. I find Christians divide into two groups: those who so stress the heavenly Zion that they have little thought for the earthly one, and those who have so much thought for the earthly Zion that they forget the heavenly one. Which group do you belong to? At a great celebration, I recall hearing the words of a song which declared that: you have come to Jerusalem; you are standing within the gate; you have come to Zion. Ah, but the letter to the Hebrews says that you have come to another Zion, the one in heaven: *But you have come to Mount Zion, to the heavenly Jerusalem, the city of the living God. You have come to thousands upon thousands of angels in joyful assembly, to the church of the firstborn, whose names are written in heaven. You have come to God, the judge of all men, to the spirits of righteous men made perfect* (Hebrews 12:22f, *NIV*). That is your home. God forgive us if we think more about this Jerusalem on earth than that one.

That is Zionism in the letter to the Hebrews. We have come to the heavenly Zion, and we are citizens. That is our home. We are strangers here, and so are the Jews. God has intended all of us for a better country, and another Zion. That is where I belong; that is where my passport is. And when I die (which cannot be too far ahead now), I go home. That is home, and that is where Messianic Jews are at home. This is a profound truth. Whilst God has a future for this earthly Zion, and whilst Christ is coming back to this earthly Zion — yes, we believe all that — if we are Zionists like Abraham, we are looking for another country, and a city whose architect and builder is God.

Now, let us look at what this letter says about Moses. The letter gives almost as much attention to Moses as to Abraham, and to the covenant with Moses as to the covenant with Abraham. But between the two there is an important distinction; the writer's attitude to the covenant of Moses is totally different to his attitude to the covenant with Abraham. The covenant with Abraham came with an oath and will stand for ever. The covenant with Moses did not come with an oath. In fact, Paul says in Galatians that covenant was temporary, only until the Messiah came. The biggest difference between the covenant with Abraham and the covenant with Moses was this: the covenant with Abraham offered blessing and curse to the Gentiles, the *goyim*. To those who would bless or curse Israel, God promised blessing or curse. That was the promise to the Gentiles, alongside his promise to Abraham and his descendants:

> *"I will make you into a great nation*
> *and I will bless you;*
> *I will make your name great,*
> *and you will be a blessing.*
> *I will bless those who bless you,*
> *and whoever curses you I will curse;*
> *and all peoples on earth*
> *will be blessed through you."*
>
> Genesis 12:2f., NIV

And we have lived to see that. What happens to nations that curse Israel? Sooner or later, they are cursed, and it is often sooner rather than later. But the covenant with Moses promised blessing and curse to the Jews, not to the Gentiles. And they were offered a choice at Sinai. Live God's way and be blessed more than any other nation. Do not live God's way and you will be cursed more than any other nation. The whole Old Testament illustrates the truth of that promise, and that promise has lasted right until now.

The greatest example of the curse of God on the Jew and the blessing of God on the Jew both happened within one decade in my lifetime, in the 1940s. And the Holocaust or *Shoah* was the example of one, and the establishment of the State of Israel was an example of the other.

This is the God who promised blessing and curse to the Jew, as he promised blessing and curse to the Gentile in the covenant with Abraham. This is a very sharp message — again to the Messianic Jew first, and to Christian Zionists. First, Messianic Jews need to know that keeping the Mosaic covenant, keeping the Torah, has nothing to do with their salvation. It is a free choice as to whether they keep Jewish culture or not. Observing the Sabbath, paying tithes, these are things of the Mosaic covenant, and according to Hebrews 8:13 that covenant is now obsolete — it is fading away; it has been replaced by a new covenant. People often get confused because some three-quarters of our Bible is called the Old Testament and a quarter the New, and the word 'testament' is the same as the word 'covenant', so it seems that our Bible is three-quarters old covenant and a quarter new, but that misleads us. There are five covenants in your Bible. The one with Noah, the one with Abraham, the one with Moses, the one with David and the one with Jesus, which I call the Messianic. Of those five, all are mentioned in the Old Testament, all are mentioned in the New, but only one of those five is called the Old and only one of them is called the New. Hebrews is concerned with the Old and the New. The Abrahamic covenant is not the 'Old Covenant' in Hebrews, for the Abrahamic covenant is permanent, will go on for ever, with an oath. The Mosaic covenant is the one that drops out in the New Testament, and Messianic Jews need to know this. You may keep circumcision, you may keep the Sabbath, you may keep tithing, but none of these is relevant to your salvation. Your salvation is due to faith in *Yeshua HaMashiach*.

However, circumcision is not part of the Mosaic covenant, but it is part of the Abrahamic. And Abraham was told that the only qualification, the only condition his descendants needed to be part of his covenant was circumcision. Therefore, a Messianic Jew who is circumcised has the claim to this land as well as heaven. Could I put it this way, if a bit bluntly, but it will bring it home to you? Every circumcised Jew carries the title deeds to the land inside his trousers. And I am quite serious. I am afraid this was the test in Nazi Germany. Genesis says that if anyone is not circumcised they are out of this covenant, they are not part of this people.

That is the only condition a Messianic Jew needs to be part of the Abrahamic covenant regarding the land. The rest is optional. Funnily enough, in the New Testament the big quarrel, the big question, was how can a Gentile become a follower of *Yeshua* without becoming a Jew? Paul fought like anything to keep

Gentile freedom from the Mosaic law. He teaches in Galatians: If you are circumcised as a Gentile, then you have to keep the whole Mosaic law. (All 613 commands.) No Gentile wants to be bound like that, and Paul gained our freedom. The question is: can Jews become followers of *Yeshua* without becoming Gentiles? It is the opposite decision now. And the answer is, in both cases, a Jew and a Gentile in Jesus are free, and become one new man, one new humanity. So the message for the Messianic Jew is: you can keep your Jewish culture and its practices as long as you never trust them for your salvation. They are works of the law, not works of faith. But the message for Gentile Christians is: you do not need to become like Jews. You are in *Yeshua HaMashiach* in freedom.

I am frankly disturbed at how many Gentiles are adopting Jewish culture. There are families in England that now will not worship on a Sunday but insist on worshipping on the Sabbath, which is Saturday, of course — and lighting candles for Sabbath meals and all the rest of it. It is an extraordinary development. God never wanted us to be Jews. He had plans for Gentiles to be part of his people. We do not need to dress and eat like Jews. Indeed, I find that some Jews despise Gentiles who try to pretend to be Jews. However, there is one good motivation in the New Testament for becoming Jewish in your behaviour, and it is to win Jews for *Yeshua*. And Paul said, *I become all things to all men, if by any means I can save some*. So he says to those with the law, I put myself under the law. To those without the law, I am without the law. He even circumcised Timothy so that he could be an evangelist to the Jews, at the same time that he was fighting circumcision, against the church leaders. He was flexible. And becoming like Jews in our behaviour and dress or diet, or in other ways, can be a valid thing for Gentiles to do if we are motivated by the desire to save some. We are not Jews, we are Gentiles, and we are in *Yeshua HaMashiach* along with Jews. That is the wonderful truth.

I could take this one stage further. There is, in some Christian circles, a belief that one day the temple will be rebuilt, the priesthood will be restored, and the sacrifices will be restored. Have you come across this? That is going backwards, according to Hebrews. I cannot conceive of a God who wants us to go back into all that after we have had the perfect once-for-all sacrifice in Christ. So please, do not let us as Gentiles think we have to be cultural Jews, and do not even believe that one day the Jewish cultus will be restored, with its sacrifices and the priests and the rest of it. There is already a place where the furniture and the utensils are being collected, ready for the new temple to be built. We have moved on, we are going to run the race looking to *Yeshua*. We are the people of the future, not the past. We are not going back into all that.

We have Jesus. That is better than all your angels, all your priests, all your sacrifices, and we are looking for a country that is better — the heavenly country where we all truly belong, and one day we will go home.

We must not read the New Testament in the light of the Old Testament, we must read the Old Testament in the light of the New. When you have found something better, you do not hanker after what was not so good.

To conclude, then, Hebrews was written to these Messianic Jews who, for a very practical reason, wanted to go back into the synagogue where they and their families would be safe, but they were leaving Jesus outside the camp and going back into the camp. There could never be any repentance from that dreadful decision. Even though Hebrews is a letter to Jews, let us take it as also a lesson for the Gentiles: Never go back! Do not even drift back. Do not neglect your salvation.

Therefore, since we are surrounded by such a great cloud of witnesses, let us throw off everything that hinders and the sin that so easily entangles, and let us run with perseverance the race marked out for us. Let us fix our eyes on Jesus, the author and perfecter of our faith, who for the joy set before him endured the cross . . . .

Hebrews 12:1a, *NIV*

So there is going to be big trouble, and suffering before glory. There is always suffering. If Jesus could go that way and call us to follow him, then we join him, 'outside the camp'.

5

ISRAEL IN REVELATION

We begin with some brief introductory remarks about the book of Revelation itself; for a more detailed introduction to it, see my book *Come with me through Revelation*.

There are fifteen prophetic books in the Old Testament, but Revelation is the only one in the New. It was written in Ephesus by John, the apostle who went to live there, taking Mary, the mother of Jesus, with him. That is where she and he died, and are buried. It was written around the end of the first century, when the emperor Domitian had installed an annual day which he called 'the Lord's Day', when everybody had to burn incense to Caesar on the altar and raise a hand in salute and say 'Caesar is Lord'. This was going to be the acid test of the faithfulness of the young Christian churches, because their creed was very simple: *Jesus is Lord*. They could not say 'Caesar is Lord', but they would pay for it with their lives if they did not. Now, they would find out whether Christians would stand firm. Already, by the time this book was written, martyrdom had begun, and in fact this whole book is a manual for martyrdom. The word 'martyr' originally simply meant witness, but very quickly it became apparent that to be a faithful witness to Jesus was to pay for it with your life, and the word changed in meaning from 'witness' to someone who would die for Jesus.

John wrote it down, but its style is different from John's Gospel and his three letters. That is because of the remarkable way it came about. God [the Father] gave it to Jesus, who gave it to an angel, who gave it to John, who gave it to the churches. No other book in the Bible has such a complicated origin. John simply wrote down what he saw and heard, and at times he was so awestruck with what he was seeing and hearing that the angel had to remind him eleven times to write things down. As he saw visions, John was called up to heaven, heard voices, heard choirs singing, and had to record these things in writing.

Revelation is an amazing book and its subject is very clear, from the prologue and the epilogue, and it is the return of our Lord Jesus Christ to earth. That event is predicted 318 times in your Bible. It is the one prediction that occurs far more times than any other. Revelation is about the events before, during and after the return of the Lord Jesus to this world. The theme is very clear, and it is two-fold: firstly, the world situation is going to get very much worse before it gets any better; secondly, the world is going to get much better after it gets worse. That is my outline of the book of Revelation, and you will find it divides very neatly into those two themes.

Now you would have thought that the book of Revelation was designed to prepare people for Christ's return, but it is not. It is written to prepare Christians for what must happen *before* he returns. It is to get Christians ready for the getting worse, much worse. Christians have always had trouble in the world but those troubles are accelerating and they will climax in the 'big trouble'. I used to hear testimonies years ago which impressed me very deeply as a young Christian. They went something like this: people used to say, 'I came to Jesus and my troubles were over.' I used to believe it and wonder why my experience did not fit. But now I have grown up, and now I know that my testimony is much truer to the Word of God. I came to Jesus in 1947 and my troubles began. I got baptised in the Spirit around 1964 and my troubles got worse. And those of you who know me will know the truth of this. I have been in more trouble in the last ten years than in the previous fifty! But Jesus said, *"In this world you will have trouble"*, so my life is fitting in with Jesus' promises. He talked about a time of 'great distress' coming, such as the world had never seen before. I love Jesus for his honesty. He never promised us an easy passage. He talked about a daily cross, not a cushion, and yet we seek comfort and safety. Jesus did not.

So Revelation is written to prepare Christians for the big trouble. I know you will find and hear preachers around the world telling you not to worry, you will not be in it. I honestly believe that is a false prophecy. I do not find any situation in the Bible which promises us that we shall escape the big trouble. If I am wrong, I would rather be wrong my way and tell people about trouble, and then find they do not need to get ready for it, than tell them they do not need to get ready for it and then find themselves in it. So I have put my cards on the table straight away. Right in the middle of this book, in the middle of the big trouble, the great tribulation, here is the word of the Lord.

This is a call to the saints to endure and to keep the commandments of God and to remain faithful to Jesus (14:12). That is the call of the book.

There is trouble coming, as the wheat and the tares grow together and become more clearly different, there will be increasing confrontation and conflict between the two, and we must be ready for this. As our Lord went through suffering to glory, he calls us to follow him along the same path. Christians are called to suffer and then to enter into glory.

That begins to set the scene. The book of Revelation is addressed to Christians about their future and how to be ready for it. To put it in a nutshell, this book is written to enable you to keep your name in the Lamb's book of life. That is why Jesus promises: *"He who overcomes will, like them, be dressed in white. I will never blot out his name from the book of life, but will acknowledge his name before my Father and his angels"* (3:5, *NIV*). If language means anything at all, that means that believers are in danger of having their names blotted out. It is not the *believer* but the *overcoming* believer whose name stays in. For we are not only called to endure suffering but to overcome suffering, to come out on top of it, as Jesus did. He has overcome, now we are to overcome. I asked a friend of mine some time ago, 'How are you?' He said, 'I'm very well, over the circumstances.' I said, 'Pardon?' 'I'm very well, over the circumstances.' Most of us live *under* them, but we are called to overcome, as he overcame.

Now, that is something about the setting of the book itself, and the question is: what does this book of Revelation say about Israel? Christian Zionists are often criticised for building their case on texts from the Old Testament which others say can be interpreted in different ways — and are criticised for not taking notice of both the fact that the New Testament talks about the church rather than Israel, and that the promised land does not figure in the new covenant at all. So I am showing what the New Testament says about Israel, and I build my faith in Israel's future on the unfulfilled prophecies of the New Testament, of which there are many in this book of Revelation. Incidentally, it is no coincidence that replacement theologians do not feel comfortable with the book of Revelation. It is a bit too Jewish for them!

Now, the word 'Israel' itself does not occur in the book of Revelation, though it occurs over seventy times elsewhere in the New Testament. Everywhere else, that word refers to the physical descendants of Jacob. It refers to physical Israel. It is never applied to the church. The references to Israel in this last book in the New Testament are indirect, almost incidental, but that is very impressive because when things are incidental it means that the writer takes them for granted, assuming that those to whom he is writing will agree. He does not need to argue over such things, he simply states them as beyond argument. For example, the people of Israel are clearly referred to, though not by the name 'Israel', in the book of Revelation. The twelve tribes are there in the book. Moses is there. The enemies of the Israelites, Jezebel and Balaam, are also in this book. It reads very much like a summary of the Old Testament. Not only are the *people* of Israel figuring in Revelation, but the *land* of Israel figures greatly. All the final great events that wind up this age take place in that land: from Jerusalem in the south to Armageddon in the north. The geographical background of this book is the land of Israel. But above all, the *scriptures* of

Israel play a very large part in Revelation. There are no specific quotations from the Old Testament, but there are over three hundred allusions. Again, the fact that they are not direct quotations but indirect allusions shows what is taken for granted. In fact, one of the reasons that Christians find this book so difficult to understand is that they do not know the Old Testament. If you know your Old Testament this book is neither obscure nor hidden. It is clear, it is simple, and I want to remind you that this book was not written for scholars, it was written for ordinary believers in seven churches in southwest Turkey, some of them ex-slaves, barely literate. It does not take a big mind to understand this book, but it does take a big heart.

The first passage that mentions Israel immediately plunges me into a hugely controversial area that came to the fore following the release of Mel Gibson's film *The Passion of the Christ*. It has raised a furore, especially among Jews and in Israel, yet I must tackle, as best I can and as honestly as I can, the subject of this controversy. The book of Revelation begins with an address and greetings, and then the prologue introduces the subject: the return of Jesus to the earth. Jesus' second coming, of course, will in some ways be not unlike his first going. As he went in the clouds from the Mount of Olives he will come back in the clouds to the Mount of Olives. But that going was only seen by some. Jerusalem as a whole was not aware of it happening. It was just over the top of the Mount of Olives, part way down towards Bethany, according to Luke's Gospel, near the top of the mountain. His coming back in the clouds will be totally public. At his first coming, only a few shepherds nearby realised what was happening. So his first coming and going had been quite private, but his second coming will be totally public. The sign in the sky of the first coming was a single point of light, a star, and the sign of his return will be lightning from the east horizon to the west: sheet lightning round the globe. Everybody will know something extraordinary is happening. So in the prologue it says:

> *Look, he is coming with the clouds,*
> *and every eye will see him,*
> ***even those who pierced him;***
> *and all the peoples of the earth*
> *will mourn because of him.*
> *So shall it be! Amen.*
>
> Revelation 1:7, *NIV*

This is a hugely controversial verse. I believe it is a reference to his crucifixion. It is the word in Psalm 22 which begins, *"My God, my God, why have you forsaken me?"* It continues, ". . . *they have pierced my hands and my feet"* (my emphasis). And here we have in one brief phrase two incidents or events that are at least two thousand years apart, brought together. *They* have pierced, and *those* who pierced him [two thousand years ago]. It is the same in both events. Now, this is the puzzle: Given that it is some two thousand years since they pierced him, how can they see him — whom they pierced?

Well, who actually pierced him? The answer is: one or two Roman soldiers with a hammer and nails, and they were just doing what they did almost every day. They were putting someone to death. It was their routine, it was their job. And they had simply been told to crucify this man, yet another one of the thousands of Jews they had crucified. Is it the few Romans, those Gentiles, who pierced Jesus? In fact, Jesus repeatedly prophesied that he would be handed over to the Gentiles to be crucified. I want you to notice that. I believe it was for them that Jesus prayed, *"Father, forgive them, for they know not what they do."* Luke makes that quite clear in his Gospel when he quotes that prayer, because it is in the context of a paragraph, and they nailed him and they stripped him, and they cast lots for the garments, and Jesus prayed, 'forgive them'. During the first three hours on the cross, Jesus' heart was concerned about the people immediately around him: his mother, a dying thief on another cross, and the soldiers gambling for his clothes. *"Father, forgive them. They do not realise what they are doing."* Notice this prayer means that ignorance is not innocence. We think that if we do not realise what we are doing it is not sin, but that is not the truth. It still needs to be forgiven, even if we were ignorant and did not know what we were doing. In fact, most of the sins that God has forgiven you were sins that you did not realise were sins; sins you were ignorant of until God faced you with them through a preacher, or through reading your Bible, or something else. Most of the sins we had to ask forgiveness for we did not realise at the time what we were doing, that we were breaking the law of God, that we were spurning his love, that we were provoking his anger. We did not realise, and nor did those Roman soldiers.

I believe this phrase *those who pierced him* must surely be wider than a few Roman soldiers. Who was responsible for the Roman soldiers doing that? The answer is: many people. Pilate had let them do it. He was responsible, even though he tried to say he was innocent of Jesus' blood. Annas and Caiaphas were responsible. Sixty-eight members of the seventy-strong Sanhedrin were responsible. Nicodemus and Joseph of Arimathea had not voted, but the other sixty-eight had, for his death. The crowd at his trial who gathered, the public, to witness his trial, cried out, 'We want Barabbas.' They wanted a man released who would be a terrorist or a freedom fighter, a man who would, they thought, set them free. That was their choice, so they were responsible for piercing Jesus. But it goes wider still than that. When Peter began to preach publicly, once the Holy Spirit gave him holy boldness to do so, he stood up in the streets of Jerusalem and said to every Jew in Jerusalem: *"You killed the author of life...."* Most of them were not even there when it happened. But he also writes, *"I know that you acted in ignorance, as did your leaders."* That does not mean they were innocent, insofar as they had allowed it to happen and done nothing to stop it. But then even the disciples had run away. It gets wider and wider.

Now, of course, the generation of Jews that were around at that time, whom Peter accused of killing the Holy and Righteous One, have long since gone. But here we have this extraordinary statement that at the end of history, when Jesus comes back, he will be seen by those who pierced him. From that I can only conclude that all Jews were being held responsible collectively for Jesus' death. That is not a popular thing to say now. It used to be, for the wrong reasons, but to say that today is to stick your neck right out. Yet, here it is. The very people who will see him are called 'those who pierced him'.

Of course, the New Testament makes it very clear that to deny that Jesus is the Messiah is to crucify him afresh. You will find that in Hebrews chapter six. But it is more than that. There was another prayer offered up by the people at the crucifixion: *"Let his blood be on us and on our children!"* (Matthew 27:25b, *NIV*).

And it looks as if God has taken them at their word. Now, of course, these words in Revelation are an echo of a prophecy in Zechariah:

"And I will pour out on the house of David and the inhabitants of Jerusalem a spirit of grace and supplication. They will look on me, the one they have pierced, and they will mourn for him as one mourns for an only child, and grieve bitterly for him as one grieves for a firstborn son"

Zechariah 12:10, *NIV*

When you go back to Zechariah, which is clearly being echoed, you find that the one they are piercing there is Yahweh, the God of Israel. Now, you have heard the word 'deicide' used in this connection. Deicide is to kill a *deus*, a god. Let us just unpack that very carefully indeed. In killing Jesus, they were killing God the Son. It was deicide. It did not succeed because the Father and the Spirit could not be killed. They were beyond reach. They were not human, but the Son of God was human and within reach and could be killed. But God the Father raised him from the dead three days later, and reversed the verdict. Yes, it was done in ignorance, but it was done, and it is still being done: crucifying the Son of God afresh. Why should God confront them with what has happened when Jesus comes back? Not to condemn them, but to convict them of sin and righteousness and judgement, because until we are confronted with our sin as sin, until we are faced with what we have really been doing, then we do not repent, and until we repent we cannot be forgiven. But it says here they will weep, because they will repent. That is when I believe a nation will be born in a day. That is how we were born again, when we were confronted with what we had been doing.

I cannot close this section without commenting on Christian attitudes to what I have called the collective guilt of the people of Israel for the death of Jesus. I want to say first that for two thousand years the church has taken an utterly wrong attitude to their collective guilt. They have assumed that Jesus gave us a mandate to be their judge and executioner, and we never had such a mandate. The church has hated them, persecuted them, exterminated them. Never did Jesus tell us to do that. It is his business to deal with sin, and the church should never have flung it in their faces.

In our study of Matthew, we thought of that dear lady in my church, a lovely believer, who remembered, as a little Jewish girl in Vienna, Christian children coming out of Sunday schools, and kicking her, spitting on her, and saying, 'You killed Jesus.' How dare they? But that is what we have done. We should never have done it, and we need to repent of an attitude that thought that Jesus told us: punish my people for what they did to me. That was never said. Catholics and Protestants are equally guilty. Martin Luther, frustrated because the Jews would not accept the gospel he had rediscovered in scripture as he expected them to, became angry with them. He was a bad tempered man and he preached his final sermon pleading with Germany to get rid of every Jew, and Hitler built on Luther's sermon. Now, that was all before the Holocaust and it took the Holocaust to bring the church worldwide to its senses. Suddenly the church began to ask, 'What have we done? Why have the Jews suffered more in Christian countries than they ever did in Islamic countries? What have we done?' The church, from one extreme, tumbled over to the other extreme and the equally opposite error, and began to absolve the Jews of today from any hand in Jesus' death. Vatican II led the way and made a statement that Jews today have no responsibility for what happened in Jerusalem two thousand years ago, to our Lord.

But we have not been given a mandate either to punish the Jews or to pardon them. It is God alone who can forgive sin against himself. We have no authority to do so. But what disturbs me most about these presumptuous statements of denomination after denomination is this: it assumes that the *church* has no responsibility for the death of Jesus, yet the fact is that every Gentile had a share in the crucifixion of Jesus. It was your sin and mine that put him there. What the church should have been saying after the Holocaust was, 'We are as guilty as you are, we share your guilt, our sin put him there.' It is not only some Gentiles, a few Roman soldiers, who were involved in his death, it is all Gentiles. David Pawson was also one who pierced him. Now that, I believe, is the truthful response — to say, yes, Jews have a collective guilt for the death of Jesus, and yes, we too share that guilt. That is why the text in Zechariah (*the house of David and the inhabitants of Jerusalem . . . will mourn*) changes in Revelation to *the world will weep*. The *world* will join in the tears. When the world realises what they have done to Jesus, ignoring him, treating him with contempt, dismissing him, the very Son of God who came to save us, *we* share in crucifying him afresh.

That is the first mention of Israel in the book of Revelation, and it is one that I believe we must think through very carefully, so that we do not swing to one extreme or the other as the church has done, swinging from blaming the Jews and punishing them for what they did to absolving them and saying it is alright, we are all innocent. Neither is the truth.

Let us move on now to an equally disturbing mention of Jews in the book of Revelation. The whole of Revelation is a letter to seven little churches in south-west Turkey, and they are the letters from Jesus himself. I am always troubled when people know Paul's letters better than Jesus' letters, or Peter's letters better than Jesus'. I hope you know Jesus' letters best of all. The only letters he ever wrote, as far as we know, we have in the record of scripture. Why would he write to seven little churches in Turkey? Why not to Jerusalem or Rome? If you look at a satellite photograph of Turkey, you will find it is all brown and dry, except right round the edges near the sea, but there is one circle in the southwest corner that is green as green, a very fertile area with rivers running through it to the sea. One river runs like this, and it is called the River Meander, from which every other meandering river gets its title. It is fertile, it is wealthy. Above all, a road goes through that green circle. It comes from Rome, in the west, through Greece, across the Bosphorus; it comes down to the circle and then it splits, and one road goes round one side of the green circle and one goes round by the coast, and it meets up again at Laodicea, and then it heads off again to Asia and to Africa.

It is the most important road in the world. Here is this fertile, wealthy area, astride the two little branches of the road that create a circle, and there are seven churches around that circle. And John the Apostle would travel, walk round those churches, as later he said Jesus 'walks' round your churches. The Graeco-Roman culture met eastern religion there. It was the key area in that world at that time. Whoever held that circle would hold the world. And at the time of the book of Revelation being written, Satan held that circle. Satan can only be in one place at once. (It always worries me when Christians say that Satan is at their meeting, it means it is the most important meeting in the world!) You can only be in one place at once when you are a creature, so Satan can only be in one place at once, and he has a headquarters on earth from which he goes out travelling to and fro. And his headquarters, when Revelation was written, was at the northern end of that circle, in a place called Pergamum. On the top of a huge mountain there was a huge temple to Zeus, the 'king of all the gods', and therefore to Satan. From that altar rose black smoke, day and night. Pergamum is a little town at the foot of the mountain. There you look up to that gigantic temple which is in the shape of a letter U, with pillars on three sides and lots of steps up the front. It looks like a gigantic armchair. And Jesus says, *"I know where you live — where Satan has his throne"* (Revelation 2:13).

You will not see that throne in Pergamum today if you go. It is in Berlin, in a museum called the Pergamon, and it has been moved there, stone by stone, from Turkey to Germany. Many Christians in Germany are praying that it may be moved back, and Turkey wants it back, but that is another story. Here was Satan's throne, because he knew that if he could control that fertile circle of cities he could control the world. And here there were these little second generation churches struggling. So Jesus wrote to those churches personal letters to encourage them, to criticise them, to rebuke them, to tell them what was right with them and what was wrong with them, and so that they were ready for the coming onslaught that would test their faith to the uttermost. That is the background to the seven letters to the seven churches. Furthermore, apart from Pergamum in the north, the other six churches all reflect the distance from Satan's throne. The two churches that were nearest to Pergamum were corrupted from the inside by idolatry and immorality by the spirit of Jezebel and others. The two churches that were furthest away from Satan's headquarters were simply dying. Satan did not need to bother with them. One had lost its first love, Ephesus, and the other had cooled off, and Jesus had to say to Laodicea, *"So because you are lukewarm — neither hot nor cold — I am about to spit you out of my mouth"* (3:16, *NIV*).

The nearest two churches Satan corrupted from the inside, the furthest two he did not need to bother with. It is in Jesus' letters to the two churches in between that we encounter a surprising reference to synagogues in the same towns.

Jesus makes some astounding statements about some of his fellow Jews in both letters. He says they say they are Jews, but they are not. They call themselves Jews, but they are not. They are synagogues of Satan. (See 2:9 and 3:9.) Now that is an extraordinary statement. First, he is disowning them. He is communicating that he is a Jew but they are not. He disowns them, they are not his people. That is because for Jesus, for Paul after him, and for all New Testament writers, a true Jew has to share the *faith* of Abraham as well as his *flesh* —has to be circumcised in heart as well as body. That is a true Jew. Until a Jew's heart is circumcised of the flesh and the flesh cut out, and until he shares Abraham's faith, he is not a Jew.

It is very interesting that during Jesus' time on earth he said similarly strong things. For example, there came a day in Jerusalem when the Jews came to Jesus and, in a very nasty way, said to him: we know who our father is. They were implying: you do not; you are illegitimate. That rumour was rife. How dare they say that to Jesus! *"Where is your father?"*

Jesus replied, *"You do not know me or my Father"* .... *"If you knew me, you would know my Father also."*

They said, *"Abraham is our father"*, but Jesus said, *". . . You belong to your father, the devil . . . . When he lies, he speaks his native language, for he is a liar and the father of lies."*

Read John chapter eight. It is a very moving chapter, finishing with Jesus saying, *"before Abraham was born, I am!"*

So Jesus here disowns certain Jews in Smyrna and Philadelphia, and he not only disowns them, he demonises them, and we learn that Satan is using those synagogues. Of course, we need to remember that even in twelve disciples Satan got hold of two. Judas Iscariot was taking bread and wine at the Last

Supper, and then it says that Satan entered into him. And when Peter took Jesus aside and began to rebuke him, Jesus rebuked him: *"Get behind me, Satan!"* We need to take this as a serious warning. Satan used two of Jesus' own disciples. They were Jews whom Satan used, one way or another. And here in Revelation we have synagogues of Satan, hostile to Christians.

Jews need to learn (we need to learn many things too, but I want to say this) that what they do to Christians they do to Jesus. *"I tell you the truth, whatever you did for one of the least of these brothers of mine, you did for me"* (Matthew 25:40b, *NIV*). I believe 'brothers' there means exactly what it means all through the New Testament: the disciples of Jesus — not the Jews, not the whole world, not our neighbour, but his 'brothers', his disciples. Saul of Tarsus had to find this out. On the road to Damascus, when Jesus said, *"Saul, Saul, why are you persecuting me?"* Saul could have said, 'I am not persecuting you, I am after these Christians.' But he learned in that blinding flash that Christians are the body of Christ, and that what you do to Christians you are doing to Christ, his body, and he feels it.

So, not only in condemning Jesus were they condemning God, but in persecuting Christians they were persecuting Christ. Now, let me just look at the age-long hostility between Jews and Christians and say one or two needed things about it. First, let us ask a simple question. Who started it? In the New Testament, the Jews started it; the greatest enemies of Christians were not the Romans but the Jews. The Jews used to get the Romans to do their dirty work for them, but it was the Jews who were responsible for Jesus' trial and crucifixion, and later for Paul's trial; and wherever Paul went to preach the gospel, who came along afterwards to undo the good work? It was the Jews and the Judaisers who got him into prison and got him flogged, and he had to appeal to the Roman authority to escape their clutches, an appeal that Jesus himself could not make because he was not a Roman citizen. So we have to be honest and say that not only did Jews kill Jesus but they hounded his followers, and Saul was first of all a missionary *against* Christ, left his home to go to Damascus after those Christians, but on the road he became the missionary *for* Christ.

But who continued it? We did! As soon as Christians could retaliate, they did, and took their revenge. Even before they had power to do that, they verbally, vitriolically abused the Jewish people. Preachers like St Chrysostom, he of the golden mouth when he preached the gospel, preached the most dreadful sermons against the Jewish people; and the church, as soon as it got power under Constantine, became the great persecutor of the Jew, forbade the building of synagogues, then closed them; made Jews wear yellow badges to distinguish them and locked them in ghettos. You have heard about the Crusades and Inquisition too often.

But 'Saint' Augustine taught that it is legitimate to use force, physical military force, to establish the kingdom. That is what led to the Crusades and the Inquisition. That is what led to the killing of the Jews in Cologne before the Crusaders got near the holy land. They were killing Jews in Germany on the way. It is a dreadful record of the church, and all this was totally contrary to the teaching of Christ, who taught no retaliation, no revenge, no getting your own back; turn the other cheek, pray for those who despitefully use you; bless them, do not curse them. Thus the Christians did not follow the teaching of Christ in this matter.

So even though the Jews started this hostility, the Christians continued it for centuries. Let me, then, say to Christians: we need to learn — just as Jews need to learn that in touching Christians they touch Christ — that in touching Jews we touch the apple of God's eye. Do you know what that is? It is not a Cox's Orange Pippin or a Golden Delicious. The apple in the eye is the iris. Look in the mirror and you will see an apple on end in your eye, the stalk in the middle, and the core and the rest around it. That is the 'apple of the eye', and that is why God is called the keeper of Israel. The word 'keeper' in Hebrew is 'eyelid'. God is like the eyelid of Israel, the apple of the eye. The iris is the most sensitive part of your body, the one that you most quickly feel pain in, and if anything, even a speck of dust, touches the apple of your eye, then your eyelid or 'keeper', slams down to protect your eye and remove that tiny attack. When God says that Israel is the apple of his eye, he means it. (See Deuteronomy 32:10.)

Let me now bring this up to date. For centuries the Jews have been in no position to retaliate. They meekly submitted to what Christian Europe did to them. I am amazed when I see films of them going to the gas chamber without a protest — just giving in. Have you seen that film *Fiddler on the Roof* — how they just gave in to the pogrom and moved away? Jews were in no position to get back at Christians because they had no power, they had no land of their own, they had no army — but now they have.

Again, I want to face facts with you. The seven letters to the seven churches have a much wider significance than churches in southwest Turkey in the first century AD, and most commentators recognise that. They are a mirror to the rest of church history. They are seven different types of churches. Now, one theory of the scholars which I do not hold, I am not convinced by it, is that the seven churches represent seven different phases of church history over the last two thousand years, so we are now in the Laodicean period. Have you heard that theory? The trouble is, it may be that many churches in my country are Laodicean, but in other parts of the world they are just the opposite.

I believe that these seven churches do not represent the church in time, seven periods, but the church in space, so that at any point in church history you can find a Laodicean church here, an Ephesian church there, a church like that in Smyrna elsewhere. I have been in the church in Smyrna, and it fits the letter to Smyrna exactly. They are suffering for their faith in that town, even now.

Anti-Semitism used to be racial — against Jews as a race. It is widespread in the church of Christ, but it is now taking a political form. It is anti-Israel. I plead with you, whatever opposition from the Jewish people comes against Christians, let us this time react in the way Jesus taught us. We are going to have an increasing opportunity to make a Christian response to whatever others do to us or say of us, until the day when Jewish people, too, believe in their own Messiah.

We have looked briefly at the relations between Christians and Jews which are part of the whole picture. But from chapter four we are transported into a totally different dimension, and a new perspective comes in. This book is what we call an *apocalypse*. That is the Greek word for revelation, and an apocalypse is an unveiling, a drawing back of a veil or a curtain or a drape, drawing aside and letting you see things that otherwise are totally hidden from you. No historian can write the whole history of the universe, for a very simple reason: no historian can see what is going on up in heaven, and no historian can see what is going on in the future. Both dimensions are necessary to understand what is going on down here now. Many of the things that are happening on earth are the result of events in heaven. Where is the devil this morning? Well, he may be going to and fro in the earth or he may be in heaven. He has access to heaven, as we know from the book of Job. He can go there and report, and when you get into heavenly places, in prayer and praise, you will find yourself wrestling with principalities and powers, because they are also up there. The devil is not in hell yet. He is going to be, but it is very important to realise that, if you want to understand what is happening in the Middle East here and now, you need to understand what is happening up in heaven at the same time, because it is related. There is interaction between heaven and earth.

We also need to understand the future to interpret the present. Christians are the only people in the world who know what is going to happen in the future and how the world is going to end, and it is because of that knowledge of the future, the unveiling of the future, that we can read the daily newspaper and interpret the signs of the times and see what is really happening.

So we see the whole of history now, because of the invitation to John — in prison for the testimony of Jesus and the word of God, a political prisoner on Patmos island. He is 'in the Spirit' and sees what is happening in heaven. Jesus said to John, *"I am the Living One; I was dead, and behold I am alive for ever and ever! And I hold the keys of death and Hades. Write, therefore, what you have seen, what is now and what will take place later"* (Revelation 1:18f., *NIV*). So we are into the future and into the end of our age, the winding up of history. The book of Revelation is the only source of that knowledge. So we are into a totally new perspective. From earth we are looking from heaven's point of view; from the present we are now looking into the future.

The key word in chapters three and five is 'throne'. It occurs sixteen times in these two chapters. We are in the throne room of the universe. We are seeing where it all happens, where the commands are given that brought this universe into being, and which shape history and the world in which we live.

Before we are told about the tragic disasters that are going to occur at the climax of this era of history, we are given a corrective, a picture of heaven at peace: a massive throne with an emerald green rainbow round it, and in front a glassy sea (or 'sea of glass') stretching as far as the eye can see, a sea without a ripple on it, without a wave; utter peace. It is very important that when we hear in the news of all the disasters that are coming, and about earthquakes, famines, wars and rumours of wars, that we constantly hold in our minds that glassy sea. God is on the throne, he is not surprised or shaken by anything that goes on down here. Heaven, highest heaven, is at peace. God knows what he is doing and what he is going to do, and how everything will turn out.

Around the throne are four living creatures, representing all God's creatures; and there are twenty-four elders. Each time you come to a number in the book of Revelation you must ask: what does it mean? This is the first time we have the number twenty-four and it is going to crop up again and again. To put it very simply: it is clearly two times twelve, so what could that possibly mean? I think the answer is only too obvious. When we get to the heavenly city we shall find there twenty-four names inscribed: twelve of them are the twelve tribes of Israel, and twelve of them the twelve apostles of the church. Twenty-four elders in heaven, supervising the work of God's two peoples on earth, Israel and the church. Here are the twenty-four representatives of these two peoples on earth, praising God, and using the language of the Psalms to do so:

> *"Holy, holy, holy*
> *is the Lord God Almighty,*
> *who was, and is, and is to come."*
>
> 4:8b, *NIV*

This is Old Testament language because this is the God of Israel, the God of the Old Testament, who is being worshipped in the New Testament. There must never be allowed a gap between the God of the Old Testament and the God of the New. It is the oldest heresy in history, called Marcionism after a man called Marcion who was the first to say that the God of Jesus is not the God of the Old Testament; that the God of the Old Testament is a fierce, harsh God, and the God of Jesus is a gentle, loving God; they are two different Gods, so away with the Old Testament. Interestingly enough, he also had to do away with the book of Revelation, because the God of the Old Testament and the God of the New are one and the same God. Let that never be doubted.

Alas, one of the most popular Christian writers today, whose books are selling around the world in hundreds of thousands of copies, is perpetuating that heresy. I was asked to write a Foreword to one of his books, and after I had read it I said I could not possibly do so. In it he said that Jesus came to show us the 'mother love' of God as distinct from the 'father love' of God in the Old Testament. That is heresy. The God of Israel is the Father of Jesus. *"Holy, holy, holy is the Lord God Almighty . . . ."* Heaven is worshipping the God of Israel today, and so are we.

One of the things God cannot do is to change the past once it has happened. He can change the future but not the past, because past and future are as real to God as they are to us. I am so thankful he cannot change the past. He cannot change the cross or the resurrection. It is fixed in time. As it is past, nobody can undo the work that Jesus did there. So here is the Old Testament God, the God Almighty, the holy God who was and is, and is to come, and he intends to wind up history, and that is the best news that I can give you. It means that this world is not going to go on like it is. It means that the mess we are in is not eternal. It means there is going to be an end to it, and the world is going to be put right by Almighty God. However, he has decided to delegate the responsibility of winding up history to a human being. As Paul told the Athenians, God has delegated the responsibility of judgment of the human race to a man. That is God's way. A man will wind up history, bring it to an end, and establish righteousness in the earth.

John, in the vision, senses a crisis within himself. He thinks that there is no one who can be trusted with such power and authority, no one worthy to open the scroll and break the seals. That scroll is God's final programme for this age — the events that will wind up history and bring it to a true consummation. What will happen is all written down, but it is sealed up, and those seals can only be broken by a man who is worthy to end history. But where is there such a man? John begins to weep. If we cannot find such a man, history is going to go on and on in the mess it is now. There must be someone; cannot there be someone?

Then one of the elders says to John, *"Do not weep! See, the Lion of the tribe of Judah, the Root of David, has triumphed. He is able to open the scroll and its seven seals"* (5:5, *NIV*). In the vision, John sees this man, but he sees an unusual man who looks like two animals. And it is a Jewish man. The world has despised Jews, dismissed Jews, treated them as of no account, as a lesser breed, only worth obliterating — yet it is a Jew who will end history for us!

There is one man, and only one, whom God the Father could possibly trust to bring history to an end. That is why I have no fear that somebody is going to press the wrong button and cause a nuclear holocaust that will bring history to an end. I have no fear of that because there is a finger already on the button, and it is the finger of this Jew, and he is God's man. And his qualifications are very interesting. He is both a lion and a lamb. Now, that is an unusual combination, but regrettably we tend to misunderstand it. We think that these two animals stand for majesty and meekness. We think that this man must be very strong and very weak. That is a false contrast, because the English use of the word 'lamb' is very misleading. Into our minds comes the picture of a little woolly, white animal a few weeks old, stumbling about on weak legs, and so many stained glass windows and so many tapestries and banners portray this little white lamb and a big strong lion. That is a false picture. This Lamb has seven horns. It is not a little immature lamb, it is a full-grown ram, and therefore when I preach I rarely say the 'Lamb of God', I say the 'Ram of God'. You would not like to be shut up in a room with a full-grown ram with seven horns. That is not a meek animal, it is a very strong animal.

So it is not meant to be a contrast between the king of the jungle and this weak little newborn lamb. It is a combination of a strong lion and a very strong ram. But why a *lion* and a ram? Again the Old Testament gives us the clue. One of Jacob's last dying, prophetic words to his sons was about Judah: that a lion would come from Judah who would rule with a sceptre. That is where the lion comes from, and here in Revelation John saw a lion of the tribe of Judah. This is the majesty, this is the king, the *Mashiach* promised, the King of the Jews. Then what about the ram? The ram is the sacrificial ram. Even the Passover lamb was not a little woolly white thing a few weeks old, it was one year old and that is fully grown. That is equivalent to a thirty-year-old man. And when Abraham was about to offer Isaac and was then stopped by the angel, he looked around and there was a ram, a full-grown male sheep with its horns caught in thorns, as centuries later on that very spot a full-grown man of thirty-three with his head caught in the thorns would be the provision of God, *Jehovah Jireh*.

So I want to correct this lion and lamb image. It is a lion and a ram, but what do they represent? The Lion represents sovereignty and the Lamb, or Ram, represents sacrifice. It is a combination of victim and victor. That is the picture here. And that is the picture which, to this day, many Jews find offensive and very hard to accept, so much so that some Jewish traditions, as I am sure you know, have developed a theory of two Messiahs, one a victim and one a victor: one son of Joseph, and the other son of David; a son of Joseph, the victim of his brothers' malice, and the son of David, the victor over the Philistines — and they cannot get it together.

The problem is that when Jesus, the *Mashiach*, came to Israel, they were looking for the lion. They were looking for the one who would lead them to victory over their enemies and political freedom and autonomy again, and that is why, when Jesus rode into Jerusalem just days before he died, they missed it totally. He was not coming as the lion, he was coming as the ram. And though they shouted, they did not even notice he was riding a donkey. When he comes again he will ride a horse, he is coming to make war, but the first time he did not come to make war. He did not come to give them political autonomy. He did not come as the lion of the tribe of Judah. But not noticing the donkey, they waved their palms and put their coats in front of the path, and shouted, *"Hosanna, Hosanna!"* And we sing that as if it is a nice little greeting, a kind of heavenly word of praise. It is nothing of the kind. 'Hosanna' means: Liberate us now! We want you to be a freedom fighter now. Set us free now. So he rode into Jerusalem and turned left instead of right. On the right was the Roman garrison, on the left was the temple, and Jesus took a whip and he whipped Jews out of the temple instead of whipping Romans out of Israel. It is no wonder that within a few days the Jews chose Barabbas, the freedom fighter, because Jesus did not come the first time as the lion of the tribe of Judah. That is how he will come the second time.

He came first as the sacrifice, he comes again and we see he is the sovereign — and when a Jew can get those two together and realise the lamb (the ram) comes first, and the lion second, they can welcome *Yeshua HaMashiach*.

But there is another strange combination here. Again, it is a combination that has been offensive to the Jewish people for centuries, and still is one of their biggest problems. Not only does this man who is both lion and ram break the seals, for he is worthy, but he is both human and divine. The amazing thing is that in the rest of chapter five, John sees this lion/ram figure being praised by the elders and by the creatures in heaven with the same words that were used in chapter four of the God of Israel. This to the Jew is the ultimate blasphemy: to treat a human Jew as God, to praise him, and ascribe honour and glory and power. But that is what chapter five does. So the second extraordinary combination in this figure which John sees is that this is not only lion/ram, this is God/man. It was for this very reason that Jesus was put on trial for blasphemy and condemned to death on the cross, and yet it was the truth. They could not even get witnesses to agree on his claims, so the high priest illegally challenged Jesus directly to condemn himself, out of his own mouth, which was a gross miscarriage of justice:

But Jesus remained silent.

The high priest said to him, "I charge you under oath by the living God: Tell us if you are the Christ, the Son of God."

"Yes, it is as you say," Jesus replied. "But I say to all of you: In the future you will see the Son of Man sitting at the right hand of the Mighty One, and coming on the clouds of heaven."

Then the high priest tore his clothes and said, "He has spoken blasphemy! Why do we need any more witnesses? Look, now you have heard the blasphemy. What do you think?"

"He is worthy of death," they answered.

Matthew 26:63ff., *NIV*

That is why Jesus died, on a charge of blasphemy. I know they had to change the charge when the Jews passed him to the Romans, because Roman law did not have a crime of blasphemy, so they changed it to treason (that he said he was the king of the Jews).

But the real reason he died was because he implied so obviously that he was divine as well as human.

By the grace of God, believers have seen, and an increasing number of Jews are seeing, the truth about the lion/ram. We first see his sacrifice — then we see that he is both God and man, the only one who could atone for our sins. With his blood, Jesus 'purchased men for God'. A new song was sung:

> *"You are worthy to take the scroll*
> *and to open its seals,*
> *because you were slain,*
> *and with your blood you*
> *purchased men for God*
> *from every tribe and language*
> *and people and nation . . . ."*

5:9, *NIV*

We move now to chapter seven. The seals have been broken, the lion/ram, the God/man, is worthy to do this, and he cracks open each seal. As he does so, tragedy and trouble are released on the world.

This is a shock to many, in view of the 'gentle Jesus, meek and mild' picture that we are often given. Here is Jesus releasing disasters on our world. But these must take place before history can be wound up properly. He breaks the first four seals, and four horses are released.

The artist Albrecht Dürer has his famous engraved pictures of the 'Four Horses of the Apocalypse'. The key to their meaning is not in the rider but in the colour of each horse. Four different colours: white, red, black and grey/green. And these are symbols, we are told, they are not difficult to understand, we are told the meaning. White is the symbol of military aggression. Most world conquerors have ridden white horses. Napoleon did, for example. The white horse is inevitably followed by a red horse, bloodshed. That leads to famine and shortage of food, which is the colour black, the colour of flesh without food. Grey/green follows quickly, and that is disease, pestilence.

These four horses are riding through parts of the earth as I write: aggression, bloodshed, famine, disease. They follow each other, but here Jesus releases them to ride through the whole earth and not just through one or two areas or regions. I will not go into all these disasters in detail, there are twenty-one of them, some of them very reminiscent of the plagues in Egypt, even down to one which is a plague of locusts.

Now, as often, the question immediately arises: what is going to happen to God's people during all this? What is going to happen to God's two peoples — Israel and the church — during all this trouble? And we find again and again in the book of Revelation an interlude, usually between the sixth and seventh in each series, to tell us the answer to that question. The seven seals, the seven trumpets, the seven bowls of wrath, are all poured out on the world. They tell you what is going to happen to the world, but what is going to happen to the people of God? So, between the sixth and seventh seals and between the sixth and the seventh trumpets, there is an interlude in which we are told what will happen to the Jews, and what will happen to the Christians. Here again is the honesty of Jesus — he does tell us what is going to come. And when I expound these twenty-one disasters I always finish by saying: nothing worse than this is going to happen. That is good news, isn't it? It really is. I am one of those who wants to know the worst, and then I can face it. When my wife was diagnosed with a deadly form of cancer, I told the surgeon, 'Please tell me the worst. We can take it, but we need to know.' When our daughter was diagnosed with leukaemia, again we said, 'Please tell us the worst.' It is better to know the worst and then you can be ready, and you can adjust. Jesus has told us the worst that is going to happen to this world, and therefore we know that nothing worse than what we read in the book of Revelation is going to happen. But naturally we want to know what is going to happen to God's people, and so in chapter seven, between the sixth and the seventh seals being broken, we have an interlude which gives us the answer.

Here, Israel as a people comes to the forefront. Now it is obvious that God has promised all the way through scripture that at the last day of history there will still be a Jewish nation.

> *This is what the* LORD *says,*
> *he who appoints the sun*
> *to shine by day,*
> *who decrees the moon and stars*
> *to shine by night,*
> *who stirs up the sea*
> *so that its waves roar—*
> *the* LORD *Almighty is his name:*
> *"Only if these decrees vanish*
> *from my sight,"*
> *declares the* LORD,
> *"will the descendants of Israel*
> *ever cease*
> *to be a nation before me."*
>
> Jeremiah 31:35, *NIV*

It is a wonderful promise of the God who caused the sun and moon to shine and the waves of the sea to roar — only if you can stop that happening will Israel cease to be a nation before him. I do not know of anybody who has been able to stop the sun and moon shining or the waves of the sea roaring!

In Revelation chapter seven, the promise to preserve the Jewish people is spelled out more clearly and in greater detail than anywhere else in the Bible, and this is the passage we are going to look at now. It is very specific. All previous predictions of the preservation of the Jewish people are in general, national terms. But here it is spelled out in such detail that the tribes are mentioned, and this is the first time in the Bible that God reveals that he will preserve the twelve tribes. As we noted in our study of Matthew, there has been much speculation about the ten lost tribes, but God has not lost them!

Then we notice that numbers are mentioned and these are a bit of a surprise. Whether these figures are to be taken absolutely literally, or are round numbers to be taken in general terms, I do not know — I will find out when it happens. But it certainly is a large but limited number of Jews, and they will be sealed by God, which means he will protect them from other human beings. We are now in the big trouble, the great tribulation, the very last days, and here are 12,000 from each tribe making a total of 144,000 Jews, who are sealed by God. Did you know that he began that practice with Cain, putting a seal on Cain's forehead to protect him from other human beings? The seal of God means: this is mine, do not touch. Just as God protected the Hebrew slaves in Egypt when the plagues came on Egypt, so he is here promising to protect a large but limited number of Jews of all twelve tribes during the troubles ahead. They will be kept on earth for God, and from those troubles.

Is there any hint as to which Jews he will select for this protection? Because it is certainly not going to be all of them, not millions. There is a very interesting little phrase applied to them: they are called 'servants of God'. The 'seal' is not the seal of the Holy Spirit, it is not the seal of salvation; they are not yet saved, but they are sealed for protection by God during the big troubles that will hit our world. They will be kept secure during that time. But who are they? I am just speculating now, but when they are said to be people who have served God, I have the feeling that this does indicate they will be religious Jews. The believing Jews, of course, are in another category. We will come to that later. But I believe that these are people who are seeking to serve God, and there are many Jews who are sincerely doing this. They may be doing it with zeal and without knowledge, and are trying to establish a self-righteousness of their own, as we saw earlier, in our study of Israel in Romans (particularly Romans chapter ten), which never works. But a man who is trying to achieve self-righteousness at least knows that God wants righteous people. He is not playing games with God, he is sincere.

There was such a man, called Saul of Tarsus, a Pharisee of the Pharisees; as touching the law, blameless. He was going all out for self-righteousness because he knew that God was righteous and needed a righteous people, and he was utterly sincere in that, though he was utterly mistaken, because the quest for self-righteousness is, as we have seen, self-defeating. It finishes up with more pride than you began with. But there is hope for such a person who is seeking to be righteous before God, but only when they come to the point when they realise that self-righteousness is offensive to God, and by faith receive God's righteousness instead, repenting even of their self-righteousness and accepting God's righteousness. As we noted earlier, that is the gospel of God. I am not ashamed of the gospel, it is the power of God for salvation to everyone who goes on believing, for in it is revealed a righteousness from God. The good news is, you will never make yourself righteous, but God can make you righteous. The righteousness of God is received by faith. So I have the feeling that these protected Jews in the big trouble will be those who are seeking to serve God because they believe that God is the centre of life. Oh yes, they will be brought through to a realisation that that is not the way, but they are sincere in seeking it.

Now, by contrast — and I only touch on this because our subject is *Israel* in Revelation — in the second half of chapter seven we are told what will happen to Christians, Gentile believers from every kindred, tribe and tongue. This is a much larger number, so big that John cannot even count them. He sees them, but he does not see them protected on earth. They are not sealed on earth. The amazing truth is that a certain number of Jews will be protected on earth, but Christians will not be protected in the big troubles. Thousands of them will suffer and die. We have noticed already that a great many people are being killed each year because they are Christians: it is over a quarter of a million annually. If you ask where that is happening, find out about Indonesia, southern Sudan, northern Nigeria, and you will realise that there are more martyrs today than there have ever been before. But in the big trouble there will be even more.

We have noted that Revelation is a manual for martyrs, to get us ready to die for Jesus. It is one thing to be willing to live for him, it is another to be willing to die for him. Now, your heart may be saying, 'I do not know if I could.' I once said to a dear, elderly saint, 'I do not know if I would have the courage to go to the lions rather than deny Jesus.' And he gave me a word of wisdom which I have never forgotten. He said, 'David, if you are faithful in little things now, he will give you the grace when the big thing happens.'

So what is going to happen to Christians? John sees this great number of Gentile believers. They have washed their robes and made them white in the blood of the Lamb, so we know they are Christian believers. Where are they? They are in heaven, not on earth. And how did they get there? Now, I want you to notice very carefully, because this passage is so often misapplied: *"These are the ones coming out of the great tribulation"* (see 7:14). It does *not* mean these came out before it happened, but it means they are coming out of it now. In simple English: you cannot come out of something if you have not been in it already. They have been *in* the great tribulation. They have suffered. They have been martyred. They have been hurt cruelly, they have wept tears. The verb tense used in the original Greek means 'coming out' ($\dot{\varepsilon}\varrho\chi\acute{o}\mu\varepsilon\nu o\iota$). It signifies coming out gradually, one by one. The coming out is a process. One by one, a great stream of people are leaving the great tribulation and finding themselves in heaven where they are being comforted, where even the sun will not smite them with its fury, as in one of the plagues that is coming on the world.

They are where God will wipe away every tear from their eyes, where he will shepherd them and care for them. And this is a contrast to the tears they have wept and the suffering they have been through. Here is an extraordinary truth when we put these two pictures together. Many people have been taught that Christians will never be in the big trouble, but that the Jews will. But here in this chapter the Jews are protected from the big trouble, even on earth, while the Christians are not protected but land up in heaven, where God comforts them after all their affliction. What a picture! But that is my understanding of chapter seven.

What is going to happen to those Jews? They will be sealed and protected on earth, and the winds of harm which will blow will not touch them. What is going to happen to believers? They are going to suffer greatly, even to the point of death, but they will come out in a steady stream of martyrs and find themselves gloriously in heaven, and God wiping away their tears. We need to be ready for this. Already in one of the churches in southwest Turkey they had had their taste of martyrdom with a church member called Antipas, who was their first martyr — not the first martyr for the faith (that was Stephen), but the first martyrdom in the seven churches. Martyrdom was going to increase, and continue to increase.

The next passage we look at really opens the second half of the book of Revelation. From now on, the attention is focussed on the *place* called Israel. The place has not been mentioned so far, only the people. But now the geographical centre of the last few chapters of Revelation is the *land* of Israel. Everything important happens here. Those who know the future know that it is centred on the Middle East. So from the demographic approach we turn to the geographic approach. John is still seeing into the future, and this is the second interlude — now between the sixth and the seventh trumpets.

In chapter eleven the focus is on two martyrs, two men who die for Jesus. Only two, but they are two very special people. John, in the vision, was told to do two things. Firstly, he is told to eat a scroll on which is written further revelation, and it tasted as sweet as honey, but his stomach turned sour. It had been sweet to chew but sour to digest. I have a similar reaction to the whole book of Revelation. It is a lovely book, it is sweet to read; to read that Jesus wins is sweet — but, as you digest it and think about all the things that have to happen before he does, it becomes sour.

In the vision, John is told to, *"Go and measure the temple of God and the altar, and count the worshippers there."* We are not told the results of that survey. It may be that he did not find any temple or any people, we do not know. We just know that he was commissioned to go and assess the religious life of the city of Jerusalem. Now, why should he have to do that, at this stage, between the sixth and the seventh trumpets? The answer lies in what was happening in Jerusalem, and we are told in chapter eleven that Jerusalem will be trampled by Gentiles. I cannot fit chapter eleven into the past. I cannot find any past situation which fits this description. Therefore, it is still future; and the time of Gentiles trampling on Jerusalem has not finished. It means that 1967 was a foretaste but not a fulfilment. It means that the trampling of this city by Gentiles is still yet to come. And it identifies not only Gentile occupiers of that city, it identifies their head, who is now in control of Jerusalem, and he is the Antichrist, the beast. We will say more about him later when we get to chapter thirteen, but here he is ruling Jerusalem, with Gentiles trampling it.

Jesus had said, *"Jerusalem will be trampled* [exactly the same word] *on by the Gentiles until the times of the Gentiles are fulfilled."* (See Luke 21:24, *NIV*.) It is not fulfilled yet. And here we have a future event in which Jerusalem is trampled, but not only is it again in bondage it is also in moral decadence. It is given two nicknames, 'Sodom' and 'Egypt'. What names to apply to the holy city of God in Jerusalem! It is as if two notorious situations in those two places are now in the capital. That city, occupied by Gentiles, ruled by the beast, in moral decadence, can well be imagined.

It is into a situation of decadence and immorality that God sends his final two prophets to warn the people. It is a situation which in a sense parallels that to which Jesus himself came, and here we have two witnesses. Why two? Quite simply because two witnesses establish the truth, according to Jewish law. You need two people to say the same thing, and these two witnesses with great courage walk the streets of a Jerusalem that is 'Sodom' and 'Egypt' (decadence and bondage), and they preach the truth of God. How bold! There has been much speculation as to who they are. They are not named. We do not know who they are. People have said it is Moses and Elijah again. I do not think so because, although they are like Moses and like Elijah, they have mortal bodies, whereas Moses and Elijah only appeared visibly on the Mount of Transfiguration, and they were not reincarnated. No, these are two unknown prophets. I will tell you who they are when they come. But they are witnesses, they prophesy in the streets of the city of Jerusalem at this climax in its history, at this consummation of history and the big trouble. They have power to call fire from heaven, like Elijah. They have power to bring plagues, like Moses. They wear sackcloth. They are able to shut off the rain for those three and a half years of the big trouble, as Elijah did.

They are prophets in the mainstream of Old Testament prophets. And yet they are also believing Jews. It is made quite clear that Jesus is their Lord, so here we have at the climax of history two witnesses, believing Jews, the Messiah's prophets, the last to be sent to Jerusalem. They are killed by the beast, their bodies are left unburied, and their fate is totally different from Moses and Elijah. Moses was not killed and nor was Elijah, but these two will be, and it says nobody will even bury them. Their bodies will be left lying in the streets — the ultimate disgrace for a Jew, not to be buried. Jesus nearly suffered that. But here there will be no Joseph of Arimathea to put that right. And there they lie. Perhaps the Jewish people in Jerusalem dare not bury them, or perhaps they do not want to, and certainly the beast and his fellow Gentiles will not want to, so their corpses are left. Three days later, what happened to their Lord happens to them: these two are given the public vindication of being raised in front of the people and they are taken straight to heaven. That is followed by an earthquake, killing seven thousand inhabitants of the city, reminding us of the earthquake at the time of Christ.

It is absolutely clear that although the name 'Jerusalem' is not mentioned in chapter eleven, it is that city, because it is said to be the great city and the holy city, and it was the city where their Lord was crucified. So that is yet another event that is to happen there before the Lord Jesus comes back. In the next chapter (twelve) we are told what will happen to the Christians at that time.

So the *place* called Israel has now come into the picture, and from now on that place is prominent. In other words, all the major end time events of our history happen there. That is a surprise to some Christians. The people and the place are linked eternally. Throughout the Old Testament, the place called 'Israel' and the people called 'Israel' are as one. Even when they are no longer living in the land, they are identified by it. They are in exile, they are in dispersion, yet their identity depends on this land, whether they live in it or not, which is why their familiar greeting even now is 'next year in Jerusalem'. You cannot define a Jew simply by his blood or his DNA. You define a Jew by the place to which he belongs, by the promised land.

When anti-Zionists constantly say that there is no mention of the promised land in the New Testament, they mean by this that there is no repetition of the link between the people of God and the holy land. Of course they admit that the four Gospels all have their context in that land. They freely admit that all the most important events on which our salvation is based happened there: it was there that Jesus was born; it was there that he was baptised; it was there that he taught and did his miracles; it was there that he was arrested; it was there that he was humiliated; it was there that he was crucified; it was there that he was raised, and from there that he ascended to heaven. Whilst admitting all that, it is then alleged that, as you work through the New Testament, those roots in this place are all pulled up. The book of Acts starts it all, and the attention is drawn away from the promised land. You could entitle the book of Acts 'How they brought the good news from Jerusalem to Rome via Antioch and . . .' but the focus of attention shifts from the Jewish world to the Gentile world, and the book finishes with Paul experiencing the rejection of the gospel by the Jews, and saying, 'I turn to the Gentiles', and it is the third time he has said that. The epistles are not written to the holy land at all. There is no epistle to Jerusalem. There is one epistle to Hebrews (believing Jews who have accepted Christ, as we have seen), but clearly it is written to Jews in Rome, not Jews in the holy land. In this way, the anti-Zionists suggest that the whole focus of the New Testament has taken us away from

Jerusalem, away from the Jewish people, into the Gentile lands and the church which has replaced Israel as the chosen people of God.

I am sure you have heard all that before. But actually, as I pointed out when we studied Romans chapter eleven, the land is mentioned because there, in that amazing chapter which speaks of the future of Israel, there is one mention of the past: that the gifts of God to the patriarchs are irrevocable — they will never be removed, never taken back. What were the gifts to the patriarchs? Well, top of the list was the land, and that verse by itself alone in the New Testament would tell us that the New Testament faith is still linked here, but it is the book of Revelation that brings the place called Israel right back into focus: the New Testament begins there and it ends there. The major events that will wind up this age, and bring Christ back, all happen within the promised land.

So we bear in mind that reminder of the background, and we have noted that Revelation chapter eleven was the first mention of the place of Israel, with its mention of Jerusalem. For the rest of this book, this is where we are. But was Revelation chapter eleven the *last* mention of the people of Israel? It could be, but maybe not.

We must now move into chapter twelve. Scholars say that this is the most difficult chapter in the whole of Revelation to understand, and therefore to explain and apply, and certainly there have been gallons of ink spent on discussing it. What is happening? What is this picture a sign of? It is called a 'sign' and a sign always points to something outside itself, something beyond, something that you need to be told about. John saw a sign in heaven, but actually it is pointing to an event on earth. What is this event? What is happening? Where is it happening? As we have seen, one of the disconcerting features of the book of Revelation is that it is constantly shifting from earth to heaven and back again. You never quite know whether you are down here or up there. That is because what happens up there affects what happens down here. That is why no history, no newscast, can ever tell you the whole story, because all they can tell you is what is happening down here, but what happens down here is a reflection of what is happening up there. The outlook of the book of Revelation is: there is trouble down here because there is war in heaven. The Bible is a unique book of history. Not only does it tell you what has happened right at the beginning, but it also tells you what is going to happen at the end, and not only does it tell you what happens down here, but it also tells you what happens up there. The Bible is the only book of history that gives you the whole story, and it is precisely because heaven and earth are interwoven in God's actions and purposes that the book of Revelation keeps shifting from one to the other.

Now we are up in heaven looking down, then we are

down on earth looking up. And *where* is this chapter? Then there is an argument about *when* this chapter happens. Has it already happened? Is it yet to happen? But of course the big question is: *who* is involved?

At first sight, it is a very simple sign. There are three characters involved. There is a woman, an unborn child and a dragon. It really ought to be quite simple, shouldn't it? Who is the dragon? Who is the woman? And who is the baby? But that is where our difficulties begin. At first impression, people say the baby boy is obviously Jesus and he is about to be born, and the dragon is the devil who is going to destroy him, and the mother is therefore Mary, and for centuries this was the Roman Catholic understanding of this picture. In other words, this is a flashback to Jesus' birth and the fact that Satan tried to destroy the baby Jesus by killing all the boys in Bethlehem. It is a well known motif in scripture. You think again of the destruction of all the boys in Egypt when Moses was about to be born, another act of Satan trying to destroy God's deliverer. That interpretation is why all over southern Europe you will see statues of the Virgin Mary crowned with twelve stars around her head, usually suspended so they look as if they are independent, but they are resting on her head, and that is why the European Union flag is twelve stars against a blue background. This was the influence of the Christian Democratic party in Germany, and it is saying that Mary is not only the Queen of Heaven, but she is the Queen of Europe. Did you think the stars represented the states in the European Union? There were already fifteen states when the twelve stars were put on the flag, and now there are many more. No, those stars represent Mary's crown against the blue of heaven. I will leave that with you, to decide whether you put it on your car number plate or not.

The Protestant reformers were so appalled by the worship of Mary and the place given to her — so that in every Catholic church, as you went in, you got an impression of a dead Christ and a living Mary, and you prayed to her — the Protestants reacted against that and said that the mother here could not be Mary. So who did they say it was? They said it must be Israel, that this is what we call a corporate figure, a woman representing a larger group of people, and of course throughout the book of Revelation every woman represents a company of people, even a city, but never an individual. In the rest of the book of Revelation, we have a filthy prostitute and a pure bride, neither of whom is an individual woman. They represent on the one hand Babylon, on the other the new Jerusalem, but here the mother, they said, represents the nation of Israel that produced Jesus.

There is something wrong with both those interpretations and it is simply this: Revelation is not about the events of two thousand years ago. When it was written, it still was not the events of sixty years before, because

Revelation was written about 90AD. It would have been an irrelevant piece of information — suddenly to be told about Jesus' birth in a book about the future, and in a section of that book which is about the last few years of this age. Why suddenly have a vision of Bethlehem? It does not make sense.

This woman is clearly someone or many 'someones' in the last final years of what has come to be called the big trouble, or the great tribulation. She is in a period called *a time, times and half a time*, or in simple English three and a half times, and quite clearly three and a half years, because later in the chapter she is in the period of 1,260 days, which is exactly three and a half years. Elsewhere in Revelation, it is described as forty-two months. This is the final time of distress such as the world has never seen before and will never see again — as Jesus called it, the time of the big trouble — the time of the great tribulation. She is in this period, therefore it is not Mary and it is not ancient Israel, that rules that quite out. I hope you are still with me because I am going to try and tell you who it is. Actually, I believe that none of these three characters is an individual: the woman is not, the baby is not, and the dragon is not. Now, just a minute, the dragon is: *that ancient serpent called the devil or Satan* (see 12:9), but that ancient serpent only had one head, and this tells us that the dragon now has seven heads and seven horns, and a whole lot of other features on his head. This is not *just* the devil but is a satanic corporation, a satanic coalition of world rulers under the control of the devil.

I do not believe that the mother is an individual person, but this is where we must face two possibilities. Just let us look at the plot a little more closely. The baby cannot be Jesus, I believe, even though he is destined to rule the nations with a rod of iron, because in this case the baby is snatched up to heaven as soon as it is born. There is no mention of a life of ministry or a death or a resurrection. There is no mention of whether the dragon actually kills the baby or not. As I will show you in a moment, the indications are that he did. So where are we now? Supremely, of course, this is wrong timing. This is not the middle of history, when Jesus was born, but the very end of history, before he returns, so the mother is not Mary, the baby not Jesus, and the dragon not just the devil. The seven heads, seven crowns and ten horns all represent rulers with power, royalty; and this dragon starts in heaven but finishes on earth, and here is the most astonishing revelation: that this dragon has already dragged a third of the stars of heaven and thrown them down to earth.

What is all that about? The 'stars' here are angels, but when they follow the devil and they are cast down on this earth, they become what we call demons. A demon is nothing but a fallen angel following Satan. Here is a dragon that already had a third of the angels of heaven under his control. What a revelation! What power! He has persuaded angels that they are better off under him on earth than staying in heaven under God. Perhaps that is why the book of Hebrews tells us that there is no hope for a rebellious angel; that Jesus did not die for angels, that his blood cannot get them back to heaven. That makes me amazed: that Jesus would die for me, but not for angels; that he would want rebel humanity back in heaven, but not rebel angels, perhaps because they have already seen what it is like and rejected it. There is perhaps no hope of them wanting it again. But now this devil himself, this angel called Satan who has access to heaven (who is in heavenly places, not in hell — read the book of Job), is now thrown out of heaven to earth and joins the demons he has already sent here. He is on earth with a deadly coalition of human rulers, he has now got more followers from among human rulers, he now has seven of them, ten crowns, and they are all in his hands.

Do you remember how Jesus was once offered the post of Antichrist? In the temptations, Jesus was offered by the devil all the kingdoms of the world, implying that they were his to give. Jesus did not argue, he did not say they are not, because he knew they were. God has allowed Satan to be the god, prince and ruler of this world, or as John says in his letter, we know that we are of God and that the whole world lies in the grip of the evil one. This world is described by Jesus himself as Satan's kingdom.

So Satan managed to persuade a third of the angels to rebel and follow him, and here at the end of history he has persuaded a corporation of earthly rulers to be his kingdom. That is the dragon in chapter twelve.

As to the woman there are two possibilities and I acknowledge them both. I will put them both to you, but I will make it quite clear which one to me is more convincing. Many Christians will tell you that this woman is Israel and that she has to flee to the wilderness, as it indicates, to survive, and that God takes care of Israel in the wilderness during the time of the big trouble. What kind of evidence is produced for this view? Well, one to me is very tenuous, and it is the fact that the woman is clothed with the sun, she is standing on the moon, and she has twelve stars around her head; and appeal is made to Genesis, where in Joseph's dream he saw the sun, moon and stars. Actually he saw a sun, a moon and eleven stars and in his dream they all bowed down to him. Joseph is described in the Bible as the man without any faults whatever. I can find only one — tactlessness. To tell a dream like that to the rest of your family, and tell your father that he is the sun and your mother that she is the moon and your eleven brothers that they are eleven stars, and that they all have to bow down to you, is a little tactless! It is not a way to win friends and influence people. But people say: therefore the sun, moon and stars of Joseph's dream symbolise the later nation of Israel. But they were purely symbolic of his family. There is no hint in the rest of scripture that this is referring to sun, moon and stars as a picture of Israel as a nation, so I am afraid that does not impress me.

Secondly, I find no evidence whatever in chapter twelve that this is about Israel.

Therefore I believe it is a picture of the church in the last days, that she is the mother, still fertile, still bearing children, and it is those new children that this satanic coalition is determined to wipe out.

Before I say more about the baby, let us say more about the mother. Her existing children are called the rest of her offspring. This baby to be born is not her first baby. She is already a family woman, and here she is with some children whom the dragon will get, and some who will flee with her to the wilderness and be taken care of by God during the big trouble. All this points me to the church at that time, which will include Gentiles and Jews, but she is the mother church of those for whom God is Father. Therefore, the baby signifies those born in those times of trouble.

If the enemy thinks that by killing the 'baby' he is populating hell, he is doing the exact opposite, he is populating heaven. The baby is snatched up immediately to heaven, replacing the devil thrown out. Why do I think that? Because it is there in chapter twelve. They love not their lives unto death. They are celebrated in heaven for being willing to die for Jesus.

Remember, the whole of Revelation is to teach people how to die for Jesus. It is full of martyrs, but the glory is that the minute the dragon kills the 'male baby' of the church, the martyr is in glory. A friend of mine was threatened by muggers with a knife in the streets of Sydney, Australia, and the man said, 'Give me your money or I am going to kill you.' My friend knew he meant business, and he simply said to him, 'All you can achieve is to get me in heaven a bit early' — and the man was so astonished by his courage that he dropped the knife and became a Christian.

The brothers *did not love their lives so much as to shrink from death* (See 12:11). It is a celebration of the martyrs at the end of our age. They go straight to heaven, where God wipes away every tear from their eyes and the sun shall no longer smite them. They are there with him. Now, what about that statement about the baby that says he will rule all the nations with an iron sceptre? That is true of Jesus, yes, but in the book of Revelation that same promise is applied to Christians, to overcomers.

"To him who overcomes and does my will to the end, I will give authority over the nations —
He will rule them with an iron sceptre;
he will dash them to pieces like pottery . . . ."

See 2:26f.

The 'baby' ('male child', *NIV*) is destined to be the ruler of the world with Jesus.

Now let me come to my last major point concerning this passage. I can respect and accept those who are convinced that this mother is Israel. It could be, and I am not going to be utterly dogmatic. I have told you the conclusion I have come to; come to your own, but do it after careful study of this whole chapter. See that everything in the chapter fits with your understanding. What I cannot cope with are those who believe the mother is Israel because, they say, it cannot be the church. Why? Because they come to chapter twelve with a preconceived negative conclusion that the church is no longer on earth, that in the big trouble the church is absent because she has already been snatched up to heaven. I need courage and grace to state this, but I believe the idea that the church will be snatched up to heaven before the great tribulation is a false prophecy.

Those who come to this passage with a closed mind, saying it cannot be the church, it must be Israel, do so because they have been under the influence of an unusual way of interpreting the Bible called 'dispensationalism'. This is a way of understanding the Bible that appeared on the Christian scene around 1830. It was an Anglican clergyman in Dublin, Ireland who was responsible. There are many theories as to where he got it from. He was the founder of the Christian

Brethren movement and a very powerful teacher, and he took very literally a text in the King James Version of the Bible which says 'rightly dividing the word of truth', and he took that word *dividing* very seriously. Actually, the word is *ploughing*. It means to open up the Bible properly, and modern versions like the New International Version say rightly *handling* the word of truth, which is much safer, but he got the idea that you have got to divide up things that appear united in the Bible, and there were three such divisions he made which have affected hundreds of thousands of people since, not just through the Brethren movement but through Pentecostals as well.

First, he divided history into seven different periods which he called 'dispensations' because in each of them God dispensed his grace and salvation in a different way. In other words, through history there have been seven different ways of being saved. After Adam, there was one way, from Cain onwards there was another way, from Noah onwards a third way, from Abraham onwards a fourth way, from Moses onwards the fifth, from Jesus' first coming a sixth, and from Jesus' second coming a seventh — seven dispensations.

Frankly, I cannot fit that into my Bible, but the second division was this, and it is so relevant to us today: he divided the Jews from the Christians forever. He called the Jews God's earthly people and Christians God's heavenly people, and God's heavenly people will live in the new heaven forever, and God's earthly people, the Jews, will live in the new earth forever, which separates us forever, it divides us. The third division was the one you are most familiar with. He divided the second coming of Christ into two comings — the first, the second and the *second* second coming. The first would be secret and would not be quite to earth, he would only reach the atmosphere, and he would then meet with the church and take the church back to heaven. A few years later he would come, and this time he would not just reach the atmosphere, he would land on terra firma.

Two second comings, not just one, and this led to three remarkable changes proposed in Christian belief. First, it meant that Jesus could come back at any moment because there was nothing in prophecy that should happen before his first *secret* second coming (and therefore he could come tonight, even at this moment). It is called the 'any moment imminent' theory of his return. I do not believe that. There are things that have yet to happen before he comes back, but if you believe in two returns, then you can believe it could happen now, this minute. I hope it will happen in my lifetime — I do not want anybody measuring me up for a wooden box — but that is quite different from expecting him at any moment. I have known little children frightened into the kingdom by being told, 'You might wake up tomorrow morning and find your parents have gone and you are left behind.' That is wicked.

That was the first big change. The second big change was that eschatology became *escap*ology. I mean by this that the study of the last things became study of the great escape to which Christians can look forward. 'Others may be in the big trouble, but I won't.' That is an attitude I could never adopt.

The third change is this: it produced a 'reverse replacement' theology. By this I mean that whilst what you and I call replacement theology is the idea that the church, at the beginning of our era, replaced Israel, now we get from this school of thinking the idea that Israel is going to replace the church at the end of this age. Crazy — matching one wrong replacement theology with what I believe is another wrong replacement theology! Both, I believe, are in error. Let us get back to our Bible. This whole scheme of Darby's in England was exported to America, because Darby went there, and persuaded a lawyer called Scofield to believe it, and that lawyer produced a 'Scofield Bible', which became the most influential edition of scripture in the United States, and through America to the rest of the world.

Never, never buy a Bible with notes in it! I will tell you why. With the best memory in the world, you will not be able to remember where you read something, whether it was at the top of the page and part of the

Word of God, or at the bottom of the page and part of the thoughts of man, and the latter is where the damage is done. 'Oh, but I read it in my Bible.' You did not read it in God's Word, you read it in the comments on God's Word! I have not met a single Christian who believes that we should be taken up before the big trouble who got it for themselves from the Bible alone; because I have searched the New Testament and there is not one single verse that in plain, simple statements says you do not need to worry, you will not go through the big trouble. It is a doctrine based on inferences, on implications, on apparently logical deductions. There is not a single statement of scripture that says you will not. It is inferred and I build my faith on the plain statements of scripture rather than on inferences.

I could not tell Israel, 'You are not alone, we are with you, we will stay with you right through to the blessed future,' and then say, 'Oh, but when the big trouble comes we will leave you alone.' My Jesus said that in the world you will have great tribulation. My apostle Paul says that through great tribulation you will enter the kingdom. Let us not be flabby Christians. I would rather be wrong my way than the other. As I have said many times, I would rather tell you to get ready for big trouble, and then find it was unnecessary, than tell you not to and then find you in it.

In Jerusalem there is a line of trees commemorating the righteous Gentiles who risked their lives to save

Jews in the Holocaust, and one tree was planted there
in memory of Corrie ten Boom, who wrote in her
diary about countries where the saints were already
suffering terrible persecution. In China the Christians
were told not to worry: before the tribulation comes,
they would be raptured. Then came terrible persecution
and millions of Christians were tortured to death. Later,
Corrie heard a bishop from China admit to having
failed, declaring that they should have strengthened
people to face persecution instead of teaching them
Jesus would return first. Corrie wrote of feeling she
had a mandate to let people know they can be strong
in the Lord Jesus Christ, in training for tribulation.
She herself had been imprisoned for the sake of Jesus,
and after meeting that Chinese bishop she would write
down words from scripture to learn, and to use in time
of tribulation.

In this book we have mentioned some great hopes
of all Israel being saved, and all the blessings that will
follow for them and the world, but in this part of our
study I am telling you what must happen between now
and then. Sometimes I hear Christians pray for things
which will happen at the end to come to pass now,
immediately, but such prayer is not in line with God's
Word, his timing. I pray the ancient prayer of the church
in the ancient language of the church, *maranatha* —
even so, come Lord Jesus. I am prepared to say come
soon and come quickly, because those are scriptural

terms. I am not prepared to pray, 'Lord, come *now*' for the simple reason that he has told us in his Word that he cannot come now. He cannot come today, he cannot come this week, he cannot come this month. He cannot come this year in my understanding of the scripture. I still hope it will be in my lifetime but it is getting a little tight! I am in my seventies now, so I am just beginning to wonder: will it be in my lifetime? But what I know from scripture is that there are certain things that must happen first.

If some Christians today get terribly excited about the idea that 'now is the time', there was a church in the New Testament that had exactly the same problem. It was the church in Thessalonica. They became very excited and said now he is coming, now we have reached the climax of history; and Paul has to write a second letter to them. His first letter had been about the second coming of our Lord, but as they got over-excited they got out of God's programme and timing. In the second letter Paul reminds them that when he was with them he had told them that Antichrist must come before Christ. The man of lawlessness must appear first. Since he has not yet appeared, it is not *now*. But hopefully it will be soon. I want the Lord to come as quickly as possible!

Again I recall that it is grounds for thanking God that Jesus tells me what I am going to face. He said to the disciples, *"I have told you these things so that your hearts will not be troubled."* He does not tell us things about the future that we do not need to know and do not need to be ready for. If Christians are not going through the big trouble, then I would find it hard to make sense of Revelation chapters four to nineteen! Why would Jesus reveal to us all this big trouble if we do not have to get ready for it? It would make us gloat over those who will have to go through it. Jesus only tells us what we need to know so that we can be ready.

We come now to chapter thirteen, and probably the lowest point is depicted here — when two human beings act in such a horrible, devilish way that they are called beasts, bestial. You know them as the Antichrist and the false prophet.

The pattern for discipleship is very clear. It is through suffering to glory. Jesus called us to follow him, and he went through suffering to glory, and for the joy set before him, he endured the cross, despising the shame. That is the way we are called to go. We do not get the crown until we pick up the cross. But we are so comfortable, and so want to remain comfortable, that we seize any teaching or any hint that we will escape suffering. But when I meet somebody like Brother Yun, and others who have suffered for the Lord, I envy them. My flesh does not, but my spirit does. There is something so real about a suffering Christian. When certain Christians in Tibet were put in prison, some other Christians, in India, began to pray for them, and their whole little circle of prayer was saying, 'Lord, get them out of prison, keep them safe, keep them from harm', and so on, until the prayer came round to a little Indian lady at the end of the circle. She said, 'Lord, why did you give them the privilege and honour of suffering for you, and not us?' Then the whole prayer meeting changed from a prayer for safety and comfort, and all the things we have, to prayer that said, 'Lord, why are we not worthy to suffer for you?' Remember that in the New Testament they rejoiced that they were worthy to suffer. And in Hebrews chapter eleven it says of those who suffered that the world was not worthy of them.

We are going through these middle chapters because there is going to be suffering for Israel, for the church, for you, for me, before the wonderful end-time things we have heard about can happen. Jerusalem will be trodden down by Gentiles, especially by one particular Gentile. We hear that Jerusalem will become the capital of an evil, Gentile empire before Jesus returns. You hear some Israelis talk about Jerusalem the eternal capital and the everlasting capital of Israel, but Jesus reveals to us that that will be rudely interrupted before he gets back. That really is a bit of a shock to us.

Then two men appear at the very end of this age in Jerusalem, who take it over on behalf of Satan. This is the point at which Satan really takes an interest in the city. Man was created above the animals and below the angels, that is our place in God's creation. But there are, as mentioned above, angels — a third of them — who have now fallen from heaven, led by Satan, and have become demons, and we find here two men who fall below the animals and behave in a more beastly fashion than animals would ever behave. Some people believe in the evolution of man — that we are getting better and better, and up and up and up. I believe in the decline of man.

In chapter thirteen it is revealed that at the end of history, before Jesus gets back, the world is held in the grip of an unholy troika: Satan, Antichrist and the false prophet.

Let us consider the first beast. He is both an individual and a corporate body. We noted that Satan (in chapter twelve) had a corporate body — seven heads and ten horns. Here we have the same thing repeated. Antichrist is an individual but he heads up a coalition, again of seven heads and ten horns. The horns stand for armies, the heads for rulers of states. So here we have a man who is heading up seven states and has at his disposal altogether ten armies. One of those heads is wounded but recovers, clearly an attempt at assassination. When this happens, of course, all will be clear. We speculate now because it has not happened, and there are many scholars who speculate on the identity of this man and all sorts of other things we do not yet know. He has supernatural power, supernatural authority, and he is guilty of blasphemy, and in pride and arrogance regards himself as the great 'I am'. He will set himself up as 'god' in Jerusalem.

I recall that some time ago I was in Croatia, looking at the only Roman palace that is still occupied and used. It is a palace built by Diocletian, the worst persecutor of Christians, at the end of the third century AD. He used to live in that palace, but as I walked through it, I came to the balcony where he had stood and faced the square, and had said: 'I am god, lie down on your faces' — and everybody had to lie down on their faces and worship him as god. At the other side of the square, he built a temple to himself as god. No wonder he persecuted the Christians, because they would never have fallen down and worshipped him. That temple is now a Christian church. Diocletian was *an* 'antichrist'. There have been many, and they all share certain characteristics.

The first beast slanders God's name and God's people. We know much about this man from elsewhere in the New Testament. Jesus gave him the horrifying title 'the abomination of desolation', a title that Daniel first used, and that was fulfilled before Christ came, in a man called Antiochus Epiphanes, who in 167 BC came to Jerusalem, slaughtered pigs on the altar of the Jewish temple, filled its vestries with prostitutes, and there erected a statue of a pagan deity; and for three and a half years that man ground the Jewish people down. He was an antichrist.

Prophecies often have a double fulfilment, and Jesus says that Daniel's prophecy about the abomination of desolation will also be fulfilled at the end of history. The Antichrist will be the abomination of desolation.

Then Paul calls him the 'man of lawlessness' who sets himself up as god, in God's very temple, and recognises no law except his own will — a totalitarian tyrant.

John wrote: *Dear children, this is the last hour; and as you have heard that the antichrist is coming, even now many antichrists have come. This is how we know it is the last hour. They went out from us, but they did not really belong to us* (1 John 2:18f., *NIV*).

Interestingly, antichrists appear to start off their reigns in power by doing good, but what seems to begin well finishes very badly. Nero did many good things for the people of Rome at first, but in his last years he was covering Christians with pitch and burning them alive to light up his garden for barbecue parties. He was sewing Christians into the skins of animals, and then setting wild dogs and lions on them.

John the apostle shows us that such antichrists prefigure *the* Antichrist. It will be the same pattern. He will come in peace, and for the first part of his reign in Israel he will seem to do good. Then, very quickly, the whole thing will turn upside down and become a terrible oppression. We do not know his name, we know his number: 666. Oh, the speculation that goes on around those figures! Hollywood knows all those figures; they bring out horror films with '666' in them. Six is a number taken to represent falling short of perfection (7); and '666' is a man who falls short in every possible way.

So in the Antichrist we see a man whose number will be a clue, and when he comes you will understand that number — but do not listen to preachers who explain it now. We will understand perfectly well when this man appears, and he will have absolute control. Now there is one problem for a totalitarian regime. A dictator wants to have total control of his subjects, and that includes *religion*. A dictator can control people's bodies and even their minds, but cannot control their souls until he gets hold of them. To do that, he needs more than political acumen; he needs more than military power. To control people's souls he must have a religion as well. Therefore, Satan's tactic is to place a religious leader alongside this political leader, a false prophet, who will ensure that the people's souls are captive as well as their bodies and minds. It is a brilliant tactic and a totalitarian regime must have that.

I have studied Hitler's rise to power in Germany, and it is very interesting. In Munich he was regarded as a 'prophet', in Berlin he was treated as a 'king', but in Nuremberg, his behaviour was that of a 'priest'. The great rallies of Nuremberg were religious festivals, with himself at the centre. So he captured German souls at Nuremberg, though he captured their minds in Munich and their bodies in Berlin.

Satan's final bid for power will have a political leader at the top and a religious leader whose job it is to bring people's souls under this political tyrant, and he will do it in a brilliant way. He will do it with miracles that will deceive. He will do it by animating an image of the dictator, an image that will move and speak, which people will be required to worship — or be killed.

In many ways, he will capture people's souls and bodies. Everybody is forced to have a mark, a number on the hand or forehead, and they cannot buy or sell without that mark. That might have seemed an incredible scenario some years ago, but now it is possible in an increasingly cashless society. It is a satanic master stroke to require that unless you receive the mark you will not be able to buy any food for yourself and your children. There will be a price for not allowing that number to be on your hand or forehead, to be used at the checkout in the supermarket where people simply run their hands over the little glass panel. We learn that the Antichrist is permitted to war against the saints, and that God will not protect them against imprisonment or execution. It is a sobering picture all round.

So where will these two beasts be? It is clear that it will be in Jerusalem, the city of God. This will be the headquarters. With the other seven nations already related, and ten armies on the circumference, the city will have been taken. Paul actually tells us that, too: he talks about the one who makes himself god in God's temple. Jerusalem is the city of the temple, the city in which the last two prophets are killed in Revelation chapter eleven, with the beast already in power. I wondered how such a thing could happen. How could Jerusalem, the capital that the Jews are determined to keep for themselves forever, become the capital of this man and his cohort — the Antichrist and the false prophet? Remember that 'antichrist' does not necessarily mean 'against Christ', or even 'against Christians'. It actually means *instead of Christ*, a substitute Messiah.

This explains something about what Jesus was offered by Satan in one of his three temptations. Satan took him to a mountain near Jericho, from the top of which you can see ten different nations even today. *"All this I will give you,"* he said, *"if you will bow down and worship me"* (Matthew 4:9, *NIV*). One day there will be a man who will accept this offer, and in Jerusalem he will have his capital.

Now I could not understand this, and I thought, 'Lord, how could such a thing happen?' It seemed impossible in the light of present circumstances, and I waited on the Lord. What I want to tell you now is not dogmatic, it is simply what came to my mind. I felt that the Lord was saying, 'You have not noticed where these two beasts come from.' So I went back to my Bible and noticed for almost the first time that the first beast, the Antichrist, the man of lawlessness, the abomination of desolation, comes from the sea. But the false prophet comes from the land. I said, 'Lord, please tell me, what are you saying? Obviously these two words are both metaphorical or symbolic, because you cannot have a man marching out of the sea like some amphibian monster.' Then he showed me that 'sea' is a symbol of the 'sea of nations'. More than once in scripture, the nations are referred to as the 'sea of nations', the Gentiles, the *goyim*, whereas whenever the expression 'the land' occurs it is the land of Israel that is in mind. So here we have a combination of a Gentile and a Jew; someone from the sea of ethnic groups with someone from the land of Israel, and it seemed to me that the two final human beings that Satan will set up in his final act for his kingdom on earth could be a Jew and a Gentile working together.

How could that happen? Again, remember that I am not claiming scriptural support for this. It is a matter of 'wait and see', and you must weigh and judge it for yourself. My mind said: Suppose the Gentile, with seven nations and ten armies, makes a treaty of peace with Israel. Daniel himself talks about a seven year treaty at the very end.

But how would Jews accept such a treaty? The answer is that when you are desperate for peace and security, you are vulnerable to gaining peace at any price. I see this as the most credible scenario, that as Israel's peace and security shrinks, and they feel more and more desperate, I believe they will succumb to a peace treaty with nations around, and that the man who signs that treaty will be the Antichrist, who will bring that 'peace' and 'security' to the land. Can you see that happening? The final road map, the final compromise, the final peace agreement in the Middle East between two men: a Gentile and a Jew. It makes sense that the Jew could be a false prophet as well. Israel has produced many false prophets, and the true prophets have felt very lonely. Jeremiah was up against the false prophets, and what were the false prophets' words? What was their favourite word? I will tell you: peace; peace, when there is no peace. False prophets are constantly talking about peace when God has not given it.

Can you imagine the headlines? 'Peace and security at last in the Middle East!' The whole world will rejoice because the whole world's peace depends on this little bit of land. The whole world's history is revolving around the Middle East at the moment; what happens there already affects the world economy. There would be an agreement in place to allow these two men to take over Jerusalem. Bombings will stop, terrorism will cease — and all Israel will be at peace and enjoy that for just forty-two months, half the time of the treaty, and then the whole thing will go terribly, terribly wrong, as it has with every other antichrist. You can lay all that before the Lord in your thinking. Does it not fit everything we are reading here? I do not know whether that scenario makes sense to you, but it did to me as I meditated on all this.

In 1 Thessalonians 5, after speaking of the second coming of Christ, Paul goes on to talk about the signs of his coming; and we need not be surprised, for the Lord's coming will not be like that of a thief in the night to those who are awake and sober and watching. But to many people Jesus' coming will be unexpected, and Paul says that when everybody is crying 'peace' and 'security' then the pains will come, as on a pregnant woman.

The false prophet will produce fire from heaven and some religious Jews may think that Elijah has returned (recalling his challenge recorded in 1 Kings 18:22, though the fire in the Elijah incident was from the Lord).

What is Satan's objective in all this? Why will he use these two men to bring an apparent peace and security to the Middle East? I believe it is Satan's attempt to have his millennium on earth. It is Satan's final throw. He has been thrown out of heaven. He now only has the earth, and he is determined to establish an Antichrist and an anti-millennium and an anti-everything, knowing full well that this was God's plan that he wanted for himself. Hitler talked of his empire as a third 'reich', and he said he was building a thousand year reich. He had his millennium idea, and that millennium was gone in less than twenty years. Satan's millennium will be even shorter: three and a half years. Then the big trouble comes and there will be faithful Jews and Christians who will not worship the beast. That is when the political situation becomes a religious situation, and that is when the great tribulation begins.

There will be a day when even pregnant women, whatever their condition, will have to run. Now it is intriguing that this advice was heeded in AD70, when Titus came against Jerusalem and the people were so besieged that cannibalism broke out in the streets; they ate the bodies of their own children to survive. Believers in Jesus (mainly Jews) remembered his advice and left Jerusalem as quickly as possible, as soon as they realised what the situation was going to be. They fled across the Jordan to a town called Pela, the ruins of which you can still see, and all the believing Jews were safe. The Jews who stayed behind were slaughtered in the fall of Jerusalem.

There is coming a day when that advice will become only too relevant again, when believing Jews and believing Gentiles in Judea will be advised to get up and go as quickly as they possibly can, because their very lives will be in danger. It is pretty tough, but it is in my Bible, it is part of the Word of God — and thank God for his graciousness.

What will keep Christians faithful when the tentacles of Antichrist spread to the whole world from Jerusalem? What will enable us to overcome? Looking ahead to Revelation chapter twenty-one, we see it is recorded that John saw a new heaven and a new earth; then we read of some great promises, and we are told that, *"He who overcomes will inherit all this, and I will be his God and he will be my son"* (21:7, *NIV*). The new heaven and new earth is only open to *overcomers*. Again, I remember that I am to learn to conquer now in the little things, and God will give me grace for the big ones.

But there is something else. I believe the one thing that cures you of fear of man is the fear of God. The big fear cancels the little one. And there is a terrible absence of the fear of God in Western Christianity at the moment. When Jesus sent out his apostles, two by two, to preach and demonstrate the kingdom through healing and exorcism, he said this, *"Do not fear those who can kill your body and do nothing else. Fear him who can throw body and soul into hell."* The fear of God is directly related to the fear of hell, *and Jesus was speaking to his apostles*. He did not say, 'Go and put the fear of hell in the sinners out there', it was rather that you, if you fear hell yourself, will not fear death.

That is a profound thing to say, and the implications are enormous. It means that Christians should fear hell. Did you know that all but two of Jesus' warnings about hell were given to born again believers? The two exceptions were both to Pharisees. Never did Jesus warn *sinners* about hell! That is a surprise. He implied it, but he never directly said it. But most of his warnings about hell are in the Sermon on the Mount, which is addressed to those who may be persecuted for the gospel's sake.

I fear hell, and that is why I can preach it. If I thought I was not in danger of hell, I know my preaching of it would be offensive. The very tone would be: I am going to heaven and you are going to hell — and I could never preach like that. I fear lest having preached to others I should be cast away myself. I fear that, not abiding in the true vine, this little branch might be cut off and thrown in the fire. I fear that, going back to my old lifestyle, I could be in a worse situation than if I had never heard of the gospel (that is 2 Peter 2, by the way). Jesus taught us that if you fear hell you will not fear death. It will keep you right.

During that short period, that second part of the seven-year treaty, that three and a half years of big trouble, what will hold Christians to be faithful will be the fear of letting Christ down, the fear of denying him. Oh, for more fear of the Lord among Christians! We cannot blame society for not fearing God if we do not, because fear is not taught, it is caught. And when God's people fear the Lord, then society will catch that fear and take God more seriously. That said, I am not a pessimist, but I am a realist. I have studied the Word and asked God to show me what I need to be ready for. I certainly need to be ready for his coming, but I need to be ready for those things that are going to happen before he gets back; I need to be ready to face big trouble.

Well, here is the good news: Antichrist and false prophet will be the first human beings to go to hell. Nobody is in hell yet. Hell is being prepared for the devil and all his angels — but it is being prepared also for those who tie themselves to Satan's purposes irrevocably.

So we have the build up, and there is a final battle in the north of Israel, between the two beasts and Jesus himself. We call the battle of Armageddon the final battle, but I have news for you: it is *not* a battle and it is *not* final.

There is no fighting. Antichrist and false prophet gather their armies there. It is the obvious place to gather military forces. It is the only flat area in the whole of the hills of Israel, the obvious battleground. Megiddo has been the battleground of history. (The 'hill of Megiddo' is Armageddon in Hebrew). This was where Jonathan and Saul were slain. Napoleon marched through Megiddo. Winston Churchill, in World War II, got a team of army officers to plan the battle of Armageddon. He envisaged the Germans coming down through Crete, and the Italians coming along the North African coast, and that they would meet in the holy land. The British Army would be trapped, he thought, at Megiddo, so he planned the battle of Megiddo. Churchill knew his Bible. But, of course, the Germans and Italians were stopped before they reached there.

It will be the final gathering place of the forces who are against our Lord and Saviour. I say there will be no battle because he destroys the whole gigantic army with his tongue, with the sword in his mouth. The tongue is shaped like a Roman sword. This is not the narrow sword that is used in individual combat but the broad sword with a ridge down the middle and a double handle. A Roman soldier swinging that could keep fifty soldiers at bay, because if they got near it, it could slice their arm or their leg clean off. It could expose the bone to the marrow, and that is why the Bible says that the word of God is like a broad two-edged sword, cutting through the bone to the marrow. But there is no battle, for, *"Out of his mouth comes a sharp sword with which to strike down the nations"* (19:15). So it is with the sword of his tongue that Jesus will kill that gigantic army at Armageddon — no fighting, just a word. With a word he could curse a fig-tree and it would be dead the next morning. With a word he will destroy that entire army. But the Antichrist and the false prophet, we are told, will be taken alive, not killed. The two leaders will then be thrown into hell, even before the judgement day. That is their lot.

Satan, behind them, will be thrown into a dungeon in the depths of the earth and removed from the earthly scene so that he can no longer deceive the nations. But God has one more thing for him to do. So — only the Antichrist and the false prophet in the lake of fire, and it simply says they will be tormented day and night, for ever and ever.

Keep that in mind when the two men appear on the earthly scene. Their doom is already decided. That is how Christians cope with present pressure, they look to the future. That is how we cope with all the problems and troubles that we face now. We look ahead, and we say this momentary light affliction is nothing compared with the eternal glory to come. Somehow that puts it all in perspective. We begin to see all these big troubles as so brief and so small. But we need to be ready.

This is my version of replacement theology: that all those who were beheaded for not accepting the beast's number in that final, brief big trouble will be reigning in Jerusalem over the earth. That is a replacement worth getting excited about, is it not? The great replacement of Antichrist and the false prophet and Satan himself by the Lord Jesus and the overcomers sitting on thrones and reigning together, even with an iron rod — and peace will come to the whole earth.

I was travelling in America and had a few hours to spare in New York. So I took a yellow taxi cab and said, 'Please take me to the headquarters of the United

Nations; I have never seen it and I am interested.' So the cab took me to the UN building, in the heart of Manhattan and dropped me there. I wanted to see two things. On the one hand there is a rock, a big granite rock outside the main door, in the grass outside. And on the rock is inscribed half a verse of scripture — only half a verse, sadly: 'and they shall beat their swords into ploughshares, and their spears into pruning hooks. Nation will not lift up sword against nation, neither shall they learn war any more.' That is why the United Nations came into being. They hoped that they could achieve peace on earth, with justice and multilateral disarmament, so that all the money that is spent on bombs and mines and destructive things could be spent on food and clothes. There it is, inscribed in granite. It is a vain hope, because it is only half a verse. And the first half says when the Lord reigns in Zion, *He will settle the disputes between the nations and they will beat their swords into ploughshares* . . . . You cannot have the second half of the verse without the first half. Well, a young lady in a blue uniform showed us round the Security Council, the General Assembly Chamber, and the other areas, filled with works of art. When she reached the end of the tour, she said, 'Well, ladies and gentlemen, that is the end of the tour. Have a nice day.'

I said, 'But you have not shown us one room.'

'What room is that?'

When I told her, she said, 'Oh, that is not open to the public, you can't see that.'

'But,' I said, 'I have come a long way to see it.'

She said, 'Well, I am sorry you can't.'

I persevered, 'I have come all the way from little old England.'

So then she softened a bit and said, 'Well, go to the foyer and ask the guards if they will let you in.' So I went to the foyer and got a big American guard with a couple of pistols in his belt, and I looked up and said, 'Excuse me, but I was told that you could let me into that room.'

He said, 'Oh no, it is locked up, it is not open to the public.'

I said, 'Well I have come a long way to see it, from England.'

Relenting, he said, 'How long would you be in there?'

'Two minutes. I have heard about that room and I want to see it with my own eyes.'

At last he took a key off a hook and led me over the foyer to a little door, and he showed me into the room. It is a very small, windowless room. There is a bit of light around the edge of the ceiling so that you can just see. And there is a circle of prayer mats and prayer stools, and in the middle, is the god of the United Nations. I had heard about this but I could not believe it. I had to see it with my own eyes. I have seen it, and you must take my word for it. But others have seen it too, I think. It is a big block of cast iron, painted matt black, about the size and shape of a coffin or a casket. And people kneel and pray to that for world peace.

'How did that get here?' I asked.

They said, 'Well, when the United Nations building was opened there was no prayer room, and the first General Secretary said that we must have a room for meditation. So they built this extra little room, and then the biggest debate in the United Nations happened. It was: what shall we put in the room? Some wanted a cross, others did not want that. Some wanted flowers; adherents of another religion did not want that. And they went on . . . . What shall we put in? Finally, they got hold of a sculptor and said, "Make us something that can be an image for every god in the world." So he made this big black block so that you can look into it. And because it is not shiny, your eyes seem to go into it. And you are supposed to look into it and see whatever god you want to see.'

I did not know whether to weep or laugh. No big black block will ever bring peace and security, it will happen when the Lord reigns in Zion. He will settle all disputes with justice, and that will make peace possible because you will never have peace as long as people feel injustice and feel that they have been unfairly treated.

When Antichrist offers his false peace and security

and the Jewish people accept that and are led by the false prophet, for three and a half years I believe they will enjoy cessation of conflict. But it will not last because it is not of God. Satan can imitate; he can counterfeit. He is a master of disguise. He can dress up as an angel of light, and he and those two men will deceive all who do not know the true God. But after that, when things are at their worst and when Israel can cry out to no-one except their God, the Lord Jesus will come back to Jerusalem, and the true millennium will be here.

So we return to chapter fourteen.

Then I looked, and there before me was the Lamb, standing on Mount Zion, and with him 144,000 who had his name and his Father's name written on their foreheads. And I heard a sound from heaven like the roar of rushing waters and like a loud peal of thunder. The sound I heard was like that of harpists playing their harps. And they sang a new song before the throne and before the four living creatures and the elders. No-one could learn the song except the 144,000 who had been redeemed from the earth. These are those who did not defile themselves with women, for they kept themselves pure. They follow the Lamb wherever he goes. They were purchased from among men and offered as firstfruits to God and the Lamb. No lie was found in their mouths; they are blameless.

Revelation 14:1–5, *NIV*

The book of Revelation was given to John in two forms: visions and voices — visual and verbal revelation. As you go through the book, it is sometimes 'I heard'; sometimes 'I saw'. The eye and the ear are the two ways in which the word of God reaches us, and the two ways that this amazing book came to John the apostle. Now what did he see? He looked and he saw the Lamb. As we noted earlier in this study, I prefer to translate this into English as 'Ram'. Jesus is the Lion of the tribe of Judah and the Ram of God, both very strong pictures. He is not a weak lamb. We remember that it was in his prime that he submitted to his Father on Mount Moriah. So there was the Lamb (the Ram) standing on Mount Zion. Now the previous vision John had of the Lamb of God was of him standing on the centre of the throne of heaven, and now here he is standing on Mount Zion. This is an astonishing change of vision. It is the first hint in the visions of John that the Ram of God is coming back here, coming back to earth, back to Jerusalem.

Then he hears a song, but the song is up in heaven, and here is a repetition of history. When Jesus came to this earth the first time, as a little baby, there was singing in the heavens, and sure enough the same thing is going to happen when he comes back the second time. There will be music. Heavenly music leaves our music way, way behind. When John hears heavenly songs, he hears them like the sound of thunder, as rushing mighty waters; as a fountain; like harpists playing thousands of harps. He cannot describe the heavenly music. Now it is coming from a choir of 144,000. I have never heard a choir that big on earth, though in heaven that is just a little group of songsters — but these are very special and these are those who were redeemed. Now do not get confused with the 144,000 in chapter seven. There it was Jews, here it is Christians; there it was a complete number of the Jews protected on earth, here it is the first fruits of Christians in heaven. There has been a lot of confusion over that simple fact. These are just the first fruits of the redeemed in heaven who are there because Jesus came to earth the first time, and so instead of angels singing in heaven; for his second visit, it is the redeemed who are already there because of his first visit, and they are singing about his second.

In chapters 14–16 we are shown a series of visions of angels, and each angel is flying to earth with a message for the human race, or for the Christians still on earth. We will not consider all those messages, but we will refer to two.

First there is an angel flying in mid-air between heaven and earth, calling to the human race: *"Fear God and give him glory, because the hour of his judgement has come. Worship him who made the heavens, the earth, the sea and the springs of water"* (v.7, *NIV*). Sadly, we find that that call is unheeded, and that instead of the judgements causing the fear of God, men curse God. When terrible things happen, people so often curse God. They say, 'Where is God? Why didn't he stop it? How can he allow such disasters to occur?' Men turn against God.

An angel comes and announces that Babylon is fallen; another one calls on the saints to endure, to remain faithful to God and to keep his commandments, to remain obedient; and then comes a little vision of hell, with the smoke of the eternal torment of those in hell rising for ever and ever. Again, we note that it is a warning to saints, not to sinners.

These are angels coming out of the temple, and here we must pause, because we need to hear what the next few pages tell us. Although John says these angels are coming out of the temple, by the time this book was written there was no temple in Jerusalem! We recall that the book of Revelation was written around 90 AD, and the temple had been torn down stone by stone in 70 AD, so what does he mean? He saw angels coming out of the temple with these messages — and then he explains it. The temple the angels come out of is not on earth but in heaven, and the truth I want now to tell you is that there are two Jerusalems. There is a Mount Zion here and there is a Mount Zion somewhere else, and Christians must live between the two.

In the Israel Museum of Jerusalem is a fascinating model of Jerusalem in the first century AD. It is beautiful. Every stone is there and the temple is there; it is a model of Jerusalem in Jesus' day, yet it is only a model. But in a sense, the Jerusalem you can see today is only a model, only a replica of the real thing. From the very beginning, God's earthly home has been a replica of his heavenly home. The tabernacle was made according to the pattern up there — it was a copy, a replica, a model; and, later, Solomon's temple was a replica, a model of the real thing up there; and Jerusalem itself on earth is only an echo of the heavenly city.

One of the major criticisms of Christian Zionists that the replacement people make is that they are hooked on the earthly Jerusalem, hardly ever thinking about the heavenly one. There is some truth in that criticism and I want to balance this up biblically now. We do not belong to the earthly Jerusalem, it is not our capital, it is the Jewish capital. We belong to the heavenly Jerusalem, we are citizens of heaven.

In other words we are the Christian diaspora, which is why when Peter writes his letter to Christians he writes to those who are dispersed, scattered. We are strangers and pilgrims. We do not belong here, we belong there.

Here are the two verses in scripture that we are often accused of totally ignoring, and that is why they say we are not fair to the New Testament teaching. First, from Hebrews:

But you have come to Mount Zion, to the heavenly Jerusalem, the city of the living God. You have come to thousands upon thousands of angels in joyful assembly, to the church of the firstborn, whose names are written in heaven. You have come to God, the judge of all men, to the spirits of righteous men made perfect, to Jesus the mediator of a new covenant, and to the sprinkled blood that speaks a better word than the blood of Abel.

Hebrews 12:22–24, *NIV*

So the question I must ask myself as well as you is: do I get more excited about the heavenly Jerusalem or the earthly one? Do I talk more about the heavenly one or the earthly one? The earthly one does not require faith, because you can see it, but we belong to the new Jerusalem.

There is another passage we are accused of neglecting. Paul writes in Galatians (4:21ff.) about the two wives of Abraham, Hagar and Sarah. Hagar stands for Mount Sinai in Arabia, and corresponds to the present city of Jerusalem because she is in slavery with her children; but the Jerusalem that is above is free and she is our mother. Jerusalem on earth is in slavery. Do you believe that? Paul is talking to Galatians about slavery in two ways: slavery to sin and slavery to the law, and he taught that you can go either way into slavery: into licence which is the worst kind of slavery, slavery to your own fallen nature, or you can go the other way into legalism, in which case the law becomes your taskmaster. Through the whole of Galatians he is saying the only source of liberty is the Holy Spirit. That is the freedom we stand for, and we belong to the heavenly Jerusalem, which is a city of freedom.

The earthly Jerusalem, the present city, is as Paul said, a city of slavery. You may in just a week's visit think it is the most wonderful place, but to know what Jerusalem is like you would have to go and live there. It might not seem like the promised land if you did so! Many Christians go there bright-eyed and with sentimental notions that it is a holy city, but some of them leave when they discover what it is really like. Jerusalem used to be God's dwelling place but it is no longer his dwelling place; the city of the living God is up there, and the temple has gone.

The first sign that people have vacated house is when they take the curtains down. Then you see the vacant windows, like blank eyes. The curtains of the temple were taken down the day Jesus died, and the Holy of holies was exposed empty. There was no glory there, nobody saw it, because God's dwelling place was no longer there; this is not the city of the living God. Furthermore, the earthly city of Jerusalem is a temporary city, but the heavenly city is the eternal city. The city of Jerusalem has been declared the eternal capital of Israel, but it cannot be because it is not going to be eternal, it will pass away. The eternal capital is up there and we belong to that eternal capital of Jerusalem in heaven. We who are citizens there are strangers and pilgrims down here.

We have come to the heavenly city, the new Jerusalem, the city of the living God. That is where we belong and we want to bring a bit of the heavenly city into the earthly city. Christian believers want to bring a bit of the freedom of the heavenly city into the slavery of the present Jerusalem. That is our mission.

In chapters 17–19 we are out of Israel, but I am going to allude to it briefly. Now we go to another city, called Babylon, which is the city of man. We have just seen that there are two cities of God, one in heaven, one on earth, and the heavenly one is his present location, his present residence and address. We say 'Our Father, who art *in heaven* . . .' — he is no longer in a temple or tabernacle. But there is another city in sharp contrast to the heavenly city. We shall see that the Jerusalem in heaven is likened to a pure bride, but the city of man, Babylon, is likened to a prostitute, because it is given over to money and pleasure. It is not a religious city, it is an irreligious city; it is a secular city. Cities have a bad history, they began with Cain and Lamech, they come from that line. Why is that? Cities are bad places in God's sight, and the reason is very simple: they concentrate sinners, and therefore they concentrate sin. You will find more vice and crime in a city than in the country because there is this concentration, and furthermore, people in cities become anonymous and they can sin without being seen.

Ancient Babylon has been partly rebuilt, but the Babylon in the book of Revelation is not ancient Babylon rebuilt, because it says that when it falls, the ships at sea can see the smoke of its destruction — so it is somewhere on the coast. It is certainly not papal Rome. Many of the reformers thought that Babylon was Rome and the pope was Antichrist. But it is nothing to do with that.

Babylon is a city that does not want God and therefore does not want God's people, and it becomes a city drunk with the blood of martyrs. It is a horrible story but the angel out of the temple up there comes and announces that Babylon is fallen. The centre of world commerce, the focus of world pleasure, is fallen.

This prompts another song in heaven called the 'Hallelujah Chorus'. Have you listened to Handel's *Messiah*? Magnificent! I think it is the greatest Christian musical work ever to have been written. It was written in just three weeks for the king of England, and of all the songs in it, the most uplifting is the *Hallelujah Chorus*, which was taken from Revelation chapter nineteen. It celebrates the end of all that man has achieved: the city of Babylon, the megalopolis which represents the peak of human technological achievement, and all that man has wanted without

God; the secular city of all — and it has fallen. When I hear the *Hallelujah Chorus* sung, I want to get up and shout to the audience: 'Do you know what that is celebrating? It is celebrating the collapse of the world economy; it is celebrating the closure of all the stock and share exchanges; it is celebrating the loss of your pension. Hallelujah!'

We have been introduced to four enemies of God's people in the book of Revelation, in this order: Satan, the Antichrist, the false prophet and Babylon — and now they are all removed from the scene in reverse order. Babylon is the first to fall. The next thing that happens is a vision. John sees someone on a white horse riding out of heaven. We know who it is: our Lord and Saviour, coming back to put the world right. He is called the Word of God here. He is called the *logos*. When Jesus came the first time, he was born King of the Jews, and he died King of the Jews; but on his second visit, he is not coming back as King of the Jews, he is coming back as King of kings and Lord of lords. The first time he rode into Jerusalem he came on a donkey, he came as Prince of Peace, but when you ride on a white charger you are coming to make war, and on his second visit the world is going to get a terrible shock. They are going to see Christ the killer instead of Christ the Saviour, because we shall see that one of the first things he does when he gets back is to massacre thousands of people. It is a very different picture of Jesus revealed here. Build your understanding of Jesus on the whole New Testament and not just on the Gospels. Do not build your picture of Jesus on his first coming only, build it on the second. In the first he came in mercy and compassion (though there were occasions when he showed his anger; Jesus could be so angry that he could cleanse the whole temple single-handedly), but in his second coming he is going to come in wrath.

Recall that this is the Ram, the Lion, coming back. *"He treads the winepress of the fury of the wrath of God Almighty"* (Revelation 19:15b, *NIV*).

He is coming back as a military leader to conquer all that is evil. We recall that a white horse is always a mark of war, invasion. (The white horse in chapter seven was not Jesus, but simply a white horse of war and invasion.)

Jesus is coming back. This is the scenario we have already begun to think about: an international army gathers at Armageddon. The plain of Jezreel is packed with international troops and their leaders, led by the Antichrist and false prophet. The world thinks that Jesus would not hurt a fly, but they could not be more wrong. He did not curse people when he was here the first time, but when he cursed a fig tree, the next day it was dead. The disciples remarked on that, and he said that if you had faith that big you could tell a mountain to jump in the sea and it would go! Jesus will come back with that same weapon of the tongue, and with a word that entire army will be obliterated — and the place will be full of stinking corpses, so many that nobody can bury them. That is when an angel calls to the birds of the air which will come and clear the mess. Israel is a land of birds; the sky can be full of birds, and they migrate through Israel. The birds are to pick the bones clean; it is a feast for them. It is quite a picture!

When the Antichrist, the false prophet and Satan have been consigned to hell, there will be a new world government, and at its head will be our Lord Jesus. There will be a Jew in charge of the world! And he will be assisted by his Jewish and Gentile people. His government will be one of true peace. It will not be a democracy; there will be no elections; we will be citizens of the kingdom, and the King himself makes the rules. All human needs will be met and there will be worldwide justice.

So it will be that in Jerusalem, for a thousand years, there will be a Priest and King ruling the earth in peace and justice, who is of the order of Melchizedek, Son of Abraham, Son of David, Son of Man and Son of God — Jesus. Our Lord Jesus will judge *all* mankind —everyone who has ever lived.

Heaven and earth pass away, and a new heaven and a new earth are revealed. And the Holy City, the new Jerusalem, comes down from God, shining with the glory of God. Significantly it bears the name of the old

Jerusalem, the Jewish capital. On the gates and walls will be inscribed twenty-four Jewish names, the tribes of the Old Testament and the apostles of the New (not a single Gentile one!) And there we will live, with the God of Israel and his Messiah for ever and ever and ever and ever.